MacINTYRE

ONE MAN...
FOUR LIVES...

MacINTYRE

ONE MAN...
FOUR LIVES...

UNDERCOVER

DONAL MAC INTYRE

BBC

FOR MY MOM

For reasons of security I cannot mention and thank publicly all who have helped in the preparation of this book and these investigations. There have been many people involved in this huge production and I am indebted to everyone who has shared this journey with the team and me. I would like to particularly thank all those at BBC Worldwide, BBC Documentaries, Peter Salmon and the Programme Legal Advice team for their loyalty, unswerving support and enthusiasm for the project. My journalistic and production team will be thanked personally for their unbelievable energy and dedication beyond the call of duty. They are Lisa Brinkworth, Paul Atkinson, Alex Holmes, Jonathan Jones, Mike Wakely, Margaret Magnusson, Pip Clothier, Lester Haines, Darren Stewart, Paul Robinson, Colin Barr, Ben Anderson, Mark Roberts, Louise McClean, Varsha Patel, Peter Coles, Lee Wilson, Shane and Bhupinder Kohli. To their family and friends, I apologize for having taken up so much of their time. To mine, I am sorry I haven't been there when you've needed me, but I hope to make up for it soon. I hope you'll forgive me.

Published by BBC Worldwide Limited,
Woodlands, 80 Wood Lane, London W12 0TT

First published 1999
Reprinted 1999
© Copyright Donal Mac Intyre, 1999
The right of Donal Mac Intyre to be identified as the author of this work has been asserted in accordance with the Copyright, Designs and Patents Act 1988.
The moral right of the author has been asserted.

ISBN 0 563 55138 0

Set in Sabon and Trixie-text
Printed and bound in Great Britain

CONTENTS

PREFACE   7

THE INVESTIGATIONS   12

THE DIARY   24

EPILOGUE   220

PREFACE

Journalism is too small or too distant a word to cover it. It is theatre; there are no second takes. It is drama – it is improvization, infiltration and psychological warfare. It is destructive. It is exhilarating, dangerous and stressful. It is the greatest job. It is my job: undercover.

I am an undercover reporter. For the past year or so, I have been a football hooligan, a care worker, a bodyguard and a fashion photographer, and this is my diary of the time in the field. It is a strange life and a difficult one. Imagine your life being divided between four cities and four different apartments. In the course of the year I have moved from theatre to theatre, from stage to stage. In the course of a day I have assumed four different personalities, worn four different wardrobes and spoken four different street dialects, and left a little bit of me behind in each of those worlds.

More important than that, though, are the experiences and emotions I've taken away with me. It's hard to put a label on them. They have seeped in and floated out of my psyche, but somewhere in the backyard of my mind the footprints of this strange work are left behind. What effect they will have on me in the long term, I have no idea. For the moment I relish the shooting gallery of challenges that this madness has offered me. In the midst of all these acting roles and journalistic expeditions I have tried not to lose too much of the real 'Donal'. I have not gone 'native' and I am still sane. At least for the moment.

In the course of any one investigation you reveal yourself in conversation and etiquette, mannerism and delivery – of thousands of gesticulations and millions of words – and cover yourself with the embroidery of many different disguises. If one stitch is loose or one word misplaced, then everything could crash, and perhaps violently so.

Certainly, as a covert operator, the journalistic safe line is a difficult one to call. Every word you utter is precious, every phrase, insinuation and gesture has to be measured and considered in legal and ethical terms. Even the cadence of your voice has to be set to appropriate rhythms according to the assumed role, the landscape and the terrain of your undercover patch.

The golden rule is this: as an undercover reporter, you must never encourage anyone to do or say anything they would not otherwise do if you had not been there. The strict guidelines within broadcasting organizations about covert filming mean that, every time I go into the field, a BBC committee or compliance officer has to grant me permission first. It's a strange but necessary experience for someone like me, who operates on instinct and intuition, but it's a marriage that works well.

The essence of the technique is getting people to tell their stories in their own words, as they would to one of their own. But this could only happen if they believe I am who I say I am, be it football hooligan, care worker, bodyguard or fashion photographer. The undercover reporter is a strange breed. There is no blueprint, no Scotland Yard course or City University module to prepare you for this kind of work. It might sound trite, but there is a sense that 'we make it up as we go along'. The only blueprint that exists is your own journalistic ethos and within those parameters you try to tread a safe line, both in terms of your journalism and personal safe-keeping. The job goes beyond normal health and safety regulations and is outside every EU working directive.

It's hard now to retrace my journey here. It reminds me of someone being asked directions in Ireland: 'Jesus, going there I'd never start from here.' If I had known where it would take me – that answer to the call – then I definitely wouldn't have started from where I did: the fifth floor of Granada's flagship headquarters overlooking regenerating urban blight, a car park called Beirut and the *Coronation Street* set.

World in Action, Granada's current affairs programme, was looking for someone to infiltrate the world of drugs. The call went around the office: 'Would the man with the biggest shoulders please stand up?' The answer to the call took me to the city of Nottingham, to investigate the realm of drug dealers.

I lived the life of a bouncer or doorman, and pretended to be a petty criminal called Tony. I entered the whispering city of grime and crime and brutality. I wasn't a grass or an informer. I was an undercover journalist.

I played Tony for eleven months and succeeded in befriending a Ferrari-driving drug dealer called Wayne. He ended up in jail. The programme's evidence led to investigations by three police forces and won two Royal Television Society journalism awards. It also earned me three death threats and a £50,000 price on my head. I had to leave the country after it was broadcast.

Of course, that's the price you pay for this kind of work. I have now joined those ranks of journalists for whom security concerns are part and parcel of their daily lives. After consultations about the potential danger to me posed by the broadcast of the investigations, I have had to leave the area I regarded as home and live in a BBC safe house. The only visitors to my bunker are work colleagues. It's not a pleasant lifestyle, but it's certainly more tolerable and much more comfortable than many London lives. I am paid well and in return have taken on all the stories in the full knowledge of the risks involved.

Why do I risk it? It is difficult to answer that question. I am not a caped crusader running about trying to arrest people in the name of journalism. I am a documentary journeyman, an archivist using covert tools. The job found me and now, four years on, it is probably the job I am best qualified to do. Ask me again in another four or five years and I might be able to tell you. For the moment I am simply grateful that this opportunity has been laid at my door – the opportunity to tell stories that journalists can't often reach.

Traditional journalistic methods don't always deliver the true and accurate picture – undiluted and unadulterated – of who and what people are. Only by seeing people speaking and operating among their own is it possible to get an accurate sense of what they're about in true documentary fashion. Undercover reporting can be the purest form of documentary – the definitive 'fly-on-the-wall'.

Though I embarked upon this journey with enthusiasm and determination, the climate in which we undertake this journalistic and documentary mission is an increasingly hostile one. It is one in which covert filming has come under scrutiny because of concerns about fakery and deception. Issues concerning privacy, the use of covert filming techniques across the media – from current affairs to the tabloid newspapers – and the way journalists work with these tools have been examined closely. I personally welcome this scrutiny.

The television series was commissioned against a backdrop of controversy – the furore over the *The Connection*, a Carlton Television programme which was discredited for its deception, and the criticism levelled at daytime chat shows such as *Vanessa* for apparently featuring hoax guests. We didn't need to be reminded that our filming and production processes would have to be rigorous, honest and transparent as far as possible.

To this end I have opened our production process up to academic study. From the start Professor Howard Tumber of City University has had unlimited access to all areas of work and has interviewed me and other members of the team at various stages. He has seen us work in the field, attended production meetings and had the opportunity to review any of the thousands of tapes shot. In time he will publish his findings. Professor Craig Mahoney of the University of Wolverhampton was similarly invited to undertake a psychological study of the pressures and strains of working undercover. He has also had the full co-operation of the team and unrestricted access to material, as well as being privy to my unguarded and private moments on and off camera. I have given him full permission to use all of this for his study.

I have been undercover in various guises for three of the last five years and, no matter which infiltration system I use, my moods, humour, frustrations and sometimes bad language are recorded in video libraries at Granada and the BBC. To live your life with a camera literally on you recording your working and off-guard moments is not normal, but I hope it hasn't changed me. It is a personal risk nonetheless. In essence it is good, old-fashioned investigative journalism but using modern tools. High-tech surveillance equipment allows me to tell the story as it really is, surrounded by its own props, revealing its own scars and naked sinews, and delivered in its own patois. There is no distortion and only one editorial prism – mine. There is just my hidden camera, my disguise and the diary notes I keep. While the sophisticated technology allows a visual and aural presentation of events, mentally I rely on the traditional method of pen and paper to rationalize my thoughts and make sense of all that I was involved in. This is my delivery system. This is how I tell these stories.

THE INVESTIGATIONS

Football

Jason held his crowd in rapture. He wrapped his hands around his body, to mimic a belly laugh – a ho ho ho – though his ample belly was big enough for him not to have to exaggerate. And the joke? How his mates had gone to Auschwitz and urinated on the graves of victims young and old, mocking the remains with goose steps and Nazi salutes.

Jason is a football hooligan. It is his life. He is not alone. They are on the terraces, they are on the streets and the smart ones stay on the streets and never see the inside of a jail.

A few years ago football hooliganism, as a threat to society and as an organized force, was thought to have become redundant and defunct. The sport was given a make-over, taken to the stock market and featured in upmarket magazines. The public profile was no longer the ugly face of football. But the gentrification of football did not mean the death of the hooligan; it simply meant that he became more sophisticated and devious, more organized and evasive, and more dangerous.

A journalist contact of mine suggested that I may have the wherewithal to infiltrate this world. I was not convinced. Unmoved, he suggested I should try to join the most dangerous of hooligan mobs: the Chelsea Head-hunters. I was even less convinced. The Chelsea Head-hunters, the most notorious of the hooligan gangs according to our research, was still operating and continuing to extend a helping hand to right-wing groups such as Combat 18 and the National Front. The investigation set out to show that, although the fighting may have left the terraces, it still takes place, mostly pre-arranged at locations outside of the scope of CCTV cameras and police surveillance. It set out to show these people as they are: racist, xenophobic and dangerous.

The Chelsea Head-hunters have slipped through the net before. Ten years earlier, eight men were freed after irregularities were discovered in records kept by undercover policemen who had infiltrated the Head-hunters as part of Operation Own Goal. Two other men who were jailed subsequently had their convictions quashed on appeal and were awarded substantial damages after doubt was cast on police statements. It was the last major attempt at infiltration into the hooligan gangs by the police.

While the police chose to rely on their recollections and notes, we decided not to leave our evidence to question. Almost every encounter was to be filmed and recorded. We would let these people convict themselves. For the first time ever, we wanted to paint an honest and detailed television portrait of who they were and what they were about.

For me, there was no more difficult role than that of an English football thug. Not only was I supposed to be a lifelong supporter of Chelsea, I had to pretend to have Neo-Nazi and ultra-right-wing politics with extreme Ulster Loyalist connections – and all this as an Southern Irishman, BBC journalist and Wimbledon Football Club supporter.

There was much work to be done before I could pass off this particular alter ego. My preparation was spent in front of the television with videos of Chelsea's greatest moments, or else nose-deep in volumes of the club history. I acquired all the paraphernalia of a psychotic fan, right down to the St George air freshener drooping from the mirror of the car. After a month's full-time study of results, goals and history, I could string together a conversation about Chelsea. Stressful examinations of my football knowledge came from taxi drivers and barmen. It was a vital grounding. Being laughed at by London cabbies was humiliating, but bore no comparison to the consequences of slipping up in front of the Head-hunters. Nothing would blow my cover faster.

We suspected that, if violence was going to erupt again, the 1998 World Cup would be a flash point. Our investigation started in

Marseilles on the day that England fans went on the rampage. We were on the ground. We had no prior knowledge, just an honest expectation that violence was going to occur. It disturbed us that we were proved so horrifically correct. It was a terrifying experience. In Marseilles I witnessed a stabbing and our producer later ended up in hospital.

The World Cup was when we first saw the Chelsea Head-hunters in a bar in Lille, snorting cocaine off a table. A BBC colleague and I looked convincing enough to be approached for more gear, for which we had to disappoint. They lost interest immediately. It was just a forty-five-second encounter, but at least we passed muster.

Jason Marriner, long-term Head-hunter, was in France, too, although I didn't see him there. He was our target; a man who was so sharp that, despite being on the frontline in the organization of football violence and on the fringes of the far right for fifteen years, he has yet to be convicted for any of those activities. I had to become his friend, his comrade. I had to become a Head-hunter.

Over the next twelve months, thousands of hours would be dedicated to making him my friend, using intricate strategies and planting clues to persuade him that I was 'one of them'. More than that, I had to have something that he might want to be a part of himself – a lucrative lifestyle. To give this impression, I adopted the guise of a drug dealer and rolled up at his local pub, techno music blaring from my £40,000 Mercedes (rented at £35 a day) and walked in carrying two mobile phones and flashing a thick wad of twenty-pound notes. The gear – Puffa jacket, baseball cap, expensive shades – and the attitude did the rest. Jason noticed me. Gradually, and with not a few setbacks, we reeled him in.

Jason Marriner was not to know it but he was to be our Trojan horse. With his friendship and our props, I forged a way through this alien world, bypassing my own terrors and multiplying my expletive count by a factor of ten. He would lead us right to the epicenter of football violence in this country. Jason's life would never be the same again. Neither would mine.

Fashion

A man tells me a story of ten men who stand over a bath where a sixteen-year-old girl waits. They masturbate over her. This is not some seedy brothel. This is Milan, the glamorous world of fashion. It's not what she dreamt of when she won her modelling contract.

Drugs, alcohol, sexual exploitation, depravity – it's not what you think of when the catwalk shines out at you from the pages of a glossy magazine. But the bright lights of fashion betray the dark heart of the industry – the dark heart that is visible to those looking from the inside out, but invisible to those looking from the outside in. The glamour and the glitz shine too brightly to allow the public an honest picture of the fashion world, a picture that may be too honest for some, too disturbing for many.

Some young girls move on unscathed by their experiences as models, but many do not. Youth, or the appearance of youth, is what sells and the industry is voracious in its consumption of nubile flesh, craving ever-younger models. But for all the innocence that the catwalks supposedly celebrate, behind the scenes these same children are exposed to a range of very brutal, adult and sometimes illegal habits. Shockingly, it is those who should protect the girls who often fail them.

We were introduced to this story by an investigative journalist who had been gathering evidence for some time, but when I got into the field the investigation took off in a direction I hadn't anticipated. From London to Paris and Milan I went undercover in the guise of a fast-talking, Irish-American photographer, supposedly taking pictures for a fashion exhibition and cover shots for a (fictitious) magazine. Despite my lack of proficiency with a camera, I managed to work my way into fashion's inner circle. What I heard and witnessed appalled me. And I am not easy to shock. I have been in crack houses, investigated drug dealers, been in the company of nakedly wicked and violent people, but what I saw shocked me to my core.

Milan, where young girls are sent by their modelling agencies to start their careers, is a city fixated by beauty. It's an ugly city fixated by beauty. Beauty and the beast. The social life is dominated by fashion seasons and collections. Because of this, 'doing Milan' is a rite of passage, an important stepping stone in a budding model's career. It is where she 'can work on her book' – that is, build up her catwalk and editorial portfolio – and, perhaps, be singled out for supermodel stardom. It is where childlike innocence careers headlong into adult depravity. Not only is fashion's dark and insidious side out in the open in Milan, it is regarded as normal. It is the spit and sawdust of normal conversation, the kernel of coffee-table chat.

In the words of a man who works for one of the world's top agencies, 'Milan is a dangerous city for young girls'. This man's job is to look after young girls, some as young as thirteen, and act as their chaperon. He used to be one of a select group of men euphemistically known as PRs or Public Relations officers. A PR's job is to find girls for rich men. They bring young models to the city's nightclubs and coax and bully them to sit at tables where wealthy businessmen, playboys and princes pay huge sums for their company. The models get no money for this. Instead, they are given free drink and, in many cases, free drugs.

I have seen models as young as fourteen being manipulated and exploited like this. Many of these girls are preyed upon by men who regard women as meat, and young models as the tenderest cut. I know, because after six months in and out of Milan I was made an honorary PR. I became a 'Moonsinner'.

The Moonsinners are the most famous of Milan's PRs and they work together, like a brotherhood. They don't just 'sell' young models to predatory businessmen. They take advantage of the girls' innocence and naiveté to seduce their way through as many conquests as possible. They have no respect or feelings for the girls. It is a sexual competition. It's a league with its own rules and points scale registering how many models they sleep with. The more extreme the sexual acts they perform, the more points they are awarded. I have heard one Moonsinner joke about continuing anal penetration when a girl asked him to stop because he had had only two penetrations and he needed ten for their 'fucking' league table. Some of the girls they admit to sleeping with have been as young as fourteen. Many of them are out of their heads on drugs and drink. Does that constitute consent?

It is not just the PRs who deal in depravity. It goes from the top down. Right at the pinnacle of the fashion industry, in the world's leading model agency, there are men who talk openly about their own drug use, who call black people 'niggers' and who share prostitutes among their colleagues. Can you believe these people when they say that your daughter is safe in their hands?

FRAUD

All is not what it seems. The tools of the fraudster and the undercover journalist are similar. All is never as it seems. But can the journalist turn over the con man? This is the challenge I set myself, this is the task ahead.

The very best fraudsters know human nature, whim and greed to doctorate level. They are street-smart, and dance and weave and bob through the human psyche to extract as much money as they can out of their chosen scam. There is no measure given or sympathy imparted – it is winner takes all. It is devious and ruthless, without compassion or remorse.

The 'magic money' scam is a huge international operation that defrauds people out of millions of dollars, year after year. No country has been immune and, despite numerous criminal investigations, the scam continues unabated. Intelligent, sophisticated and extremely wealthy men – and a few women – have lost their fortunes to it. Some have been reduced to complete penury. And yet still it continues. It continues because people are greedy and the con men are clever. In fact, the perpetrators of the scam are among the most 'competent' and prolific fraudsters operating today.

The 419 scam is a nasty, relentless business and the sting is one of the most brutal. It developed first in Nigeria and has become associated exclusively with the country. Victims who have tried to recover their money have gone missing. Some have been killed. The perpetrators are prepared to murder if you threaten their lucrative operation. In the rare cases when the scam is reported to the police, it is usually too late – all traces of it and its perpetrators have vanished and the fraudsters have moved on to entice and entrap the next round of victims.

These con men survive on their intuition, delicate timing and planning. Operations are meticulously planned to bureaucratic precision, timing is calculated with a comedian's touch and the fraud practised with delicate and surgical execution. They are good at their job.

The dynamics of financial fraud have always fascinated me and when we heard, through a contact, about this scam, I was hooked. The duality, the detail, the psychology and the drama made it a challenge I found it hard to decline.

I had read about this 'Nigerian 419 scam' before. It's a strange morality tale of greed meeting greed, where fraudster and victim mostly deserve each other. The 'marks', as they are known, aren't victims in the traditional sense – certainly not like the targets of football violence – but the tools of seduction used to entrap the marks are immoral and illegal. The challenge is to expose the con men's operation by joining it, to drive their network of fraud into extinction by broadcasting the mechanics of it from the inside out.

The scam – officially called the '419 Fraud' after the criminal code in Nigeria that it breaches – historically started out with a rash of faxes sent to businesses, purporting to come from a member of the Nigerian aristocracy or government who wants to get vast amounts of dollar reserves out of the country.

The plan involves a member of the public getting a huge commission for a small but supposedly vital bit of assistance. They are asked either to provide bank accounts for receipt of stolen funds, or to contribute just ten thousand dollars to assist in getting sums as large as one hundred million dollars out of Nigeria. A return of ten million dollars is promised for this comparatively small investment. This is their blueprint. In fact, the con mutates and evolves like low life in the primordial soup. It may sound unbelievable because it is just that. But it works. It is convincing, and hundreds of thousands are conned out of their life savings every year. On this stage, greed meets greed – it is not an edifying sight.

There is no sympathy on behalf of the fraudsters. They will get every penny, every cent. One millionaire businessman was so cleaned out that with his last pounds he flew himself and his family out to Nigeria and threw himself on the mercy of his virulent adversaries. He told them that they had bled him dry, that he was skint save for the change in his pocket. He flung himself on their mercy and asked for a job. That businessman now works with the fraudsters, defrauding other businessmen like him. He greets new marks coming off the plane in Nigeria or Ghana and prepares them to be rolled over and cooked like a pig on a spit.

All over the world marks are ripped off. Marks are no fools, but in the hands of a smart con man a mark and his money can easily be parted. And these con men are some of the smartest. They make the scam international, moving the mark from country to country, making any offence multi-jurisdictional and therefore difficult to prosecute.

One of the ways the gang promises to get the money out of Nigeria is by dyeing it black and exporting it as paper for printing. Then they get their client to pay a sum of money for the dye cleaner that will restore the bills back to their original state. In a series of 'accidental' and apparently unforeseen complications, more money is extracted from the businessman as he gets closer to his treasure-chest of millions. All the while he is consoled by the fact that, how-ever big his contribution to the scam, it is tiny compared to the prof-its he will gain. It isn't, of course. Given the chance, the merciless fraudsters will extract every penny the hapless 'investor' has.

The scam was a challenge of different proportions to the other investigations. To play this gang at their own game we were going to have to be twice as smart as the smartest fraudsters. That's a tall enough order in itself, but as an undercover journalist you face additional problems. In order to infiltrate a fraud, you may unwit-tingly be involved in defrauding someone else, thus breaking the law. To get round this, we decided that I would approach the Nigerians with a mark provided by us, who I would pretend to want to stitch up for a cut of the profits. This would allow me to throw my lot in with the gang and observe the scam at close quar-ters without sharing culpability.

We decided it was better to get caught out by the Nigerians with a big lie rather than a small one. Our plan involved inventing a 'lot-tery winner' (in reality, a retired senior police officer) whom I, as his corrupt bodyguard, wanted to fleece. If I were to con the con men, my plan would have to be as sophisticated as theirs. It would have to be sharp and credible.

Our sting on them required us to go to extensive lengths to lay the groundwork for it, including dummying up the front page of a co-operative Carlisle newspaper with a photograph in which our mark is seen receiving a cheque for £5.4 million. I wanted to show this cutting to the con men as proof of our mark's good fortune.

A meeting was scheduled through a contact. The Nigerians took the bait. I have played a bouncer before, so it wasn't difficult improvizing and looking the part – the suit, the shades, the scowl, the attitude – but Solomon, the six-foot-four fraudster, was edgy. He was eyeing my jacket, trying to work out whether I was armed.

I was – with a secret camera. Solomon himself was probably hiding something much more deadly. He had his plans. I had mine.

CARE

There is a village I know which has a large residential home for people with learning difficulties. Visitors would often remark on how integrated the local community and the residents at the home were. There was no abuse from the pavement, no cruel verbal side-swipes from kids who didn't know better. The residents were regarded with fondness and welcomed into peoples' homes and the homes and residents, in turn, shared their amenities with us.

This village is my hometown. It is where I grew up. This is why issues involving care homes have always been important to me. The lesson learned in childhood has not been forgotten. It was a lesson in compassion and humility. The lesson is an old one, but one that we forget at our own cost. You judge a society not on how it treats its most able citizens, but on how its weakest fare. Unfortunately, many of them aren't able to communicate this to us. Many can't communicate at all.

The care story is not a story about one home: it is about a system. Those recruited at the bottom end to work in these homes can be unqualified and unskilled, and many who are trained are untrained sufficiently to cope with the difficulties that their patients pose; some lack patience. The work is difficult, trying and stressful but the pay is often poor. This is the system in which the most vulnerable in society find themselves.

It is a system that has attracted much scrutiny in recent years and one that continues to require attention to ensure that patients get the standard of support, treatment and care they deserve. On the basis of information received from a source, we looked at one home that was suspected of not operating to those standards. We decided that I should go undercover to find out what conditions were really like there.

This year was the first time I have been called on to address these issues as an employee, as a player. It was a traumatic and distressing experience. Of all the stories I delved into for the TV series and book, it took up the least of my time but asked the most of me personally. It had no pyrotechnics, required no courage, won no bravery plaudits at the end. I didn't even have to alter my appearance. It was just sad. What is even worse is that, in all probability, this home was better than many. Nonetheless, it fell down badly in the standard of care delivered to its vulnerable patients. The only redeeming feature is that perhaps my exposé will help improve standards.

My investigation took place over the latter part of December 1998 and early January 1999. I got a job in a care home as a care assistant. (Details that would identify the home or the patients have been omitted.) Jobs as care assistants are not hard to find; nor are they well paid. I was greeted with open arms. After a cursory interview, I was given the job. I started work before my references were taken up and without anyone checking my records.

Most of my CV was true, but it did not mention that I had ever worked as a journalist. To them I was Mike, a quiet, friendly guy who was taking time out from the activity-holiday sector where I was a lifeguard and general sports instructor. I have done both of those things, so this was no fabrication. My only sin was that of omission. I did, though, tell them I had no experience whatsoever in the care of people with learning difficulties. I was told that special experience was not necessary because I would be trained on the job.

My first tour around the home left me with an impression as indelible as the tattoo I had recently had carved on my arm to 'qualify' as a football hooligan. It was a grey building and a grey day, but the warmth of the greetings I received from the patients lifted my spirits. Most of the residents have mental ages of young children and their affectionate, trusting behavior had a childlike sincerity that touched me. I anticipated that this was going to be a special job, one that would be more testing on my patience and on my personal qualities than any job I have ever done, but one I could embrace. And testing it was.

The hours were long and the patients were occasionally challenging, but by far the most difficult aspect I had to cope with was the casual inhumanity of the staff. It wasn't that they were brutal or cruel by nature; rather, they lacked the training, insight and experience to act any other way. It was difficult enough for me just witnessing it, but my problems were miniscule compared to the difficulties experienced by the patients.

I had only spent five days in the home when it was laughingly regaled to me how one patient was rolled up and wrapped in a carpet when he was proving hard to handle. The patient involved had a mental age of four. A worker there openly admitted that it was sometimes necessary 'to inflict pain' in order to control difficult patients so that they learned not to be disruptive again. He also told me that he had seen another care worker 'chin' a patient when he thought no-one else was looking. I began to wonder what I'd walked into.

I started work in Christmas week and it was a lonely, depressing time for me. For thirty-two years I have spent Christmas with my family, so it was a sad irony that on this particular Christmas Day, I had, for the first time, no family around me. For the patients on that day, the care workers are their only family, so I was part-family to them and they were all family to me. It was a day that I'll never forget, and never want to forget.

THE DIARY

13th April 1998

Today is the first day of the rest of my lives. Today I begin my big adventure to invade and infiltrate an eclectic collection of worlds and tell the story of the people I meet along the way. It's like my first day at school, but without the lunch box.

The plan is to be rested and relaxed and chilled out. The truth of the matter is that I *am* chilled. I have frostbite on both hands. I couldn't be happier, though. Just finished a 125-mile canoe race over the Easter weekend. I canoed from Devizes in Wiltshire to Westminster, non-stop, and am dead on my feet – and arms and legs. At the end I cried with the pain.

That was Saturday. That was play. Today is Monday – this is work. I've got frostbite, I'll survive it and, I hope, the year ahead. My adventure starts now.

17th April 1998

The request is for a series of thirty-minute programmes. Beyond that, the briefing paper is blank. There are no prescribed stories or proscribed journeys – there is only me and editor Alex Holmes and an empty folder. The task is to fill in the blanks and to join up the dots. First, though, to find the dots. The production process is going to be long and complicated and one which Alex and I start today with a view towards broadcasting in seventeen months' time. This length of time is a luxury.

'Give me those ideas that you always thought were impossible to do,' Alex Holmes says to journalists and producers on the phone. 'Give me your fantasy top-ten stories that you would love to bring to the screen.'

We are touting for ideas. Anything is possible. Broadcasting doesn't get better than this.

20th April 1998

Team-building time. It's a crucial process, more important even than the ideas. We don't want clones; we need individuals with flair, whose personalities complement each other. There will be huge stresses involved and pressures outside the normal remit of current-affairs journalism. They need to be able to hack just about anything, and be thoroughly professional about it. We cannot assume that anyone will be willing to involve themselves in some of the dangerous work we do, and plan to do; people can only ever volunteer for this type of 'work'. It's a lot to ask. It occurs to me that assuming four different personalities, and maybe more, in eighteen months may be a lot to ask of me, too. It took me a year to live the life of a bouncer – how am I going to be the doorman to four lives in just a year and a half?

25th April 1998

My frostbite is clearing up. I still can't move two fingers on my left hand, but my right hand is fine now except for some occasional tingling in the fingertips.

'You would gladly be a hypochondriac if you had the time,' a pal said to me the other day.

'There's always next year,' I replied, more in hope than expectation.

5th May 1998

Alex and I are weeding out the ideas. One is gaining currency above all others: football hooliganism. Alex is very keen on infiltrating the Chelsea Head-hunters and thinks it could be right up my street. The story comes from a producer, Pip Clothier, who is joining the team shortly. He has been looking at security issues relating to the forth-coming World Cup and offers up the Head-hunters as a potential target. In between slurps of cappuccino, I challenge the currency of the story. 'Isn't it a bit eighties? It just feels dated to me,' I say.

'Well, let's do a bit more research on this before we cast it aside.'

I agree to the wait-and-see, but personally it just doesn't have the contemporary feel.

12th May 1998

Spread out in front of me is a rogues' gallery of press photographs of some of Britain's most dangerous football supporters. They have scars, tattoos and shaved heads. It seems that there are still gangs of thugs systematically organizing fights, turf wars and revenge attacks on a weekly basis, much of which goes unreported. I can't say that I really believe it, but the information indicates as much. I question Pip Clothier. He says it's because nowadays the fighting does not take place in the vicinity of football matches, but at pre-arranged locations.

'But why the Chelsea Head-hunters? Why not the Glasgow Rangers firm or the City Governors from Manchester City?' I persist.

Pip explains his reasoning to Alex and me. 'We really ought to look at the Chelsea Head-hunters. They have been causing trouble for decades. A major police undercover operation against them in the late 1980s failed. The group is still organized and believed to be responsible for some vicious attacks. The World Cup and Chelsea European matches next year give them plenty of excuses to cause trouble.'

I consider what has been said. The forthcoming World Cup means that these hooligans may be on the offensive again. Pip is enthusiastic. 'You should use that as a starting point. Journalists haven't travelled with this gang before. They have to be seen up close and personal to be believed.'

I am still not convinced.

25th May 1998

A friend of mine tells me a horror story about a care home in England that has recently been closed down. I am reminded of the issue again.

She is a nurse and has worked in care establishments before – good ones – but she knows of some that aren't. They are slipping through the system, she says, and patients are being maltreated.

This is such a difficult subject. I decide to run the issue by the team when it is up to full complement to see if it ignites sparks in them as it does in me. Nothing disturbs me more than seeing a system abuse people who are incapable of defending themselves. It would be very satisfying if we could do something to put the care of society's most vulnerable firmly on the public agenda.

27th May 1998

'He was slashed across the neck. Repeatedly. He nearly died.'

I am being brought up to speed on what the Chelsea Head-hunters have done to a West Ham fan at the beginning of the 1996–97 season. Unsurprisingly, the victim did not turn up in court to give evidence. Other incidents are run by me. My mind switches from scepticism to confidence-crisis. If the Head-hunters are ripe for a story, can I carry it off? Hesitantly, I voice my doubt. There is a silence in the team meeting. We'll cross that bridge later.

2nd June 1998

I trawl though the bottom of my filing cabinet for all those old newspaper clippings that I promised myself I'd follow up but never did. There is one that catches my eye from a year ago. It needs more research but it could be interesting. The *Daily Mail* headline reads 'Judge's Blast at the Cheats of Nigeria' and the story goes on to say that three fraudsters were jailed after they attempted 'the magic money scam' on an American lawyer. 'The three men pretended twelve million pieces of black paper were American $100 bank notes which had been dyed so they could be smuggled out of Nigeria. They asked for an advance for a special chemical to wash away the dye. US lawyer Lester Turner, from

Harbour Springs, Michigan, was duped into handing over more than $17,500.'

Apparently five billion pounds has been stolen worldwide using this scam. If that's the case, then it is really significant. But how do I infiltrate it? I put the cutting onto my mounting research pile. We have a lot of stories to consider now. There are a number of stories that would be better covered in a more conventional fashion and we leave those to be told by a more conventional journalistic team. 'Conventional' is not what we are about. From the outset, we have been looking at the most challenging stories. As a result, we are left with the impenetrable, the impossible and the frankly unimaginable. It may be that our journalistic eyes are bigger than our bellies but, for the moment, we have time to indulge ourselves. Later, as reality bites, deadlines and logistics will probably curb our aspirations. Today is about achieving the impossible, tomorrow is about delivering what's achievable.

5th June 1998

It's decision time for the football story. The World Cup begins in five days' time. If we're going to use it as a starting point, we have to make up our minds today. Apart from the prospect of violence there, the World Cup represents the shallow end of the hooligan story. If I want to enter these waters, I must first dip my toes in and see if I can swim. Hopefully, I'll be too insignificant for them to pay close attention to me, but it will allow me to get a feel for things and observe them in action.

Several hours later, we decide to run with it. I am persuaded to do the story for a number of reasons, namely: the prescience of the World Cup, the continuing threat of violence and my personal brand of optimism that usually doesn't allow me to reflect too long on the impossibility of impossible tasks. I am off to the World Cup. I am tense. No one else seems to be showing any nerves. The tickets are booked.

We are running with the story – but can I run with them? Can I be a Head-hunter? This test lies in the field.

6th June 1998

If we are to investigate this story, then I am going to need some specific help. In order to penetrate such dangerously sophisticated realms, you need sometimes to work with people who have first-hand experience of them. Paul Atkinson is a journalist with a wealth of knowledge of worlds such as these. He will be invaluable in helping to plan strategies and devise routes into the football world and into the mind of a football hooligan.

10th June 1998

Instead of trawling through old drawers for research, today I trawl the internet. It spits out lots of information about the Nigerian 419 fraud. Just last month, apparently, the US House of Representatives was told that fifteen businessmen who went to Nigeria in search of their stolen monies were killed there. One man who went there was kidnapped by the fraudsters, and his family were sent body parts until they gave in to a million-dollar ransom demand. He was never seen alive again. His body, doused in petrol and set alight, was later found outside a leading Lagos hotel. No one was ever caught or prosecuted for the murder. This is harrowing stuff and it seems that the Nigerian Government is very slow to prosecute or arrest anyone involved in the scams. This could prove to be a very dangerous story to pursue. For now, though, it's the World Cup that must hold my focus.

13th June 1998

Stress is very hard to measure. I know that housework stresses me. I know that DIY sends me over the edge, but I don't manifest stress the way others do – or at least I don't think I do. If I did, then I couldn't do my job. In the most dangerous moments, where fear would normally take a grip and adrenaline would send your heart racing, I try to flatline it and ignore the threats; I dampen the natural inclinations towards stress and control any public demonstration of it. I express it predominantly just before I enter the fray or when I come out of the field. The most public demonstration of it is nail-biting – a nasty habit, but one that has accompanied me undercover. My other companion has been Stop 'n' Grow – which has neither stopped my nail-biting nor allowed them to grow.

My nails are my personal stress barometer. At the moment they have been eaten right back and have frayed at the edges. Tomorrow I leave Britain to become a football hooligan.

14th June 1998

The train slips out of the station and I slip out of my life as a journalist and into one as a hooligan. Eyes wide open and mouth firmly closed. This is the beginning. It is a fresh life.

Distractions are welcome. This is my first time on the Chunnel and the excitement of travelling on this man-made wonder deflects the terror and trepidation that is evident in my very quiet demeanour.

Paul notes my delicate silence and is concerned. I assure him that I am just getting my head around the headcases around me. There are fans and then there are hooligans? Right now I can't tell them apart.

It is always said of the French that they run a good train service. It runs on time and is able to cope with the most boisterous of passengers. It is, I can confirm, hooligan-resistant.

For most of the fans around me it's a journey just a little too fast to be comfortable, too short to sleep through and the train too thin for walkabout. Other than that, the ride from Paris to Marseilles is fine, though when the bar is empty and you can't smoke, even the mildest football supporter feels a little irritable.

It is not a holiday, it's an initiation ceremony on a large scale. It is important to be here to learn how football hooligans work and maybe, just maybe, to meet some Chelsea Head-hunters. I hope to bounce around their company, skirt their conversation and try to belong. In truth, though, as I sip beer in the corner of the restaurant car on the way to Marseilles, I couldn't feel more displaced.

I do not belong. Only a wave of lunatic optimism keeps my hopes alive that my team and I will crack this hooligan game and get to the heart of their psychosis and their violence. Sometimes optimism is enough. Sometimes you need self-delusion on a vast scale.

However, I have a problem. Last week I stood up in the office and confessed: I have a drinking problem. Alex, my editor and friend, was concerned enough to take me out in order to try and eliminate the problem over lunch and dinner. I've had many severe lectures, and still the doubts remain. Can Donal drink for England? The answer is 'no', but I am trying to pretend. The key, I discovered, is to take it one day at a time and, wherever possible, drink bottled lager and leave most of the contents in the bottle. More learning and more drinking – like college all over again.

Let me introduce you to the new friends I met today. Friends who are no friends of mine.

LEEDS MAN

French trains are oblivious to the attentions of Leeds man. All of us drink the train dry, singing to 'St George', but Leeds man swings to the saint and tries to smash the windows on the train. Thud THUD THUD – *and* still his head doesn't give in. The glass is impervious to his aggression.

Petrified, I hide behind the pony-tailed ticket inspector, who runs his train with more steel than any Chelsea mob. This is his train and he is having none of it. Leeds man had slept in a doorway in Calais for three days and smells grimy and grotty. The inspector takes more offence at his aroma than his outburst, and sends him to the back of the train to cool down – with all windows open.

Leeds man, before he tries his DIY frontal lobotomy, asks me which firm I run with. This is clearly not a business inter-company league he is talking about. I tell him that I run with the Chelsea. This is rehearsed. He takes offence, but as we are with England an uneasy truce is maintained.

ELLIOT, THE TICKET TOUT

A curly-haired scouse bums a fag off me, then a light and then a drink. He is entertaining and confirms every prejudice about Liverpudlians that ever exhibited itself on Harry Enfield's television show. I am just grateful to talk to someone who I don't think is going to beat me up. At least, while he's buttonholing me with his implausible tales of rich women and rock concerts, no one else pays me any attention.

BURNLEY MAN

This man is an evolutionary dead-end. Certainly it is a unique beast that runs down the Old Port in Marseilles, on the cobbled stones, in 90 degrees and against the din of police shields. He runs naked, with one of his arms aloft in a fist and the other polishing an Irish tricolour (recently burned) on his posterior, his white thighs pumping high and his fat torso swaying with lager. Defiantly he sings to the tune of 'Give Me Joy In My Heart' and taunts the line of 500 state police in their riot gear.

> Keep St George in my heart and keep me English,
> Keep St George in my heart I pray.
> Keep St George in my heart, keep me English,
> Keep me English to my dying day.

> No surrender,
> No surrender,
> No surrender to the IRA.
> SCUM!

I do not belong here. The feeling of fear and exposure is now overwhelming.

The riot police rap their shields. The English supporters, feeding on the madness of the naked man, rap nearby windows and then, hungry for action, attack the police. The locals, who take offence at this invasion, join in, attacking the fans. Mayhem. If there were a escape clause in my contract, I would enact it now.

Looking like a football hooligan and pretending to act like one – that is my job – but I still don't expect to be picked up and treated like one.

Suddenly, I am surrounded by seven riot police. Three behind me, three in front of me and one roving inquisitor. My hands shoot up. I obviously look like a perpetrator (at least that's going to plan) and I am swamped by shields and guns.

There are no eyes to implore to, some are wearing helmets while others are shrouded by controlled aggression. Threatened and under pressure, angry and frustrated at a city in anarchy, the gendarmes are in no mood for pleading hooligans. They have had enough. I am caught in the cross-fire of their anger and a random association between the clothes I am wearing and the deeds that others have done. This is the association I strove for when I set off, but not quite the desired consequences. In short my disguise wasn't supposed to be this effective. I look like a hooligan, therefore I am.

I turn to one of my colleagues, who is openly filming with a tourist video camera. He is 30 metres away, but is helpless to intervene. He can't come to my aid because it may blow my cover to the fans looking on. It's one thing talking to the police but an altogether different thing to be seen talking to a cameraman. That is a cardinal sin. A gendarme pads me down and searches my pockets.

My first day as an Englishman abroad and it looks like they are going to arrest me. About to be carted off, I protest, 'Je suis un journalist. Je suis Irlandais' – I'm a journalist, I'm Irish – and, on my first day in the field, I have to break cover to save myself a night in the cells. Thank God hooligans can't speak French.

My first search and my legs are like rubber. I'm glad it doesn't last too long and that just looking like a hooligan isn't enough to convict me as a thug. Thankfully I'm not wearing a secret camera – this is not a covert operation, but a fact-finding mission. Later, having escaped arrest, I turn back towards a café near the port where an array of expensive yachts line the quays. I have arranged to rendezvous here with the rest of the team after the near-arrest separated us. The missiles continue to fly and, under fire, my head bobs and weaves awkwardly, like an overweight Labrador. What an initiation.

Something narrowly misses my eye, but there is nowhere to run. I rush to the side of the street to hide behind a car. I don't feel much safer. It's a sea of violence, overlapping and overwhelming. There seems an unnatural order to the anarchy. Fans beside me talk of a stabbing and someone else says that an English fan has been killed. It raises the temperature.

My earlier suggestion that we (Paul, another colleague and I) crash out in sleeping bags on the Old Port quay, under the stars, is looking less sensible in the middle of this riot. My two colleagues are not impressed with me. I have to agree.

As we run for shelter down one side street off the old square, fleeing the anarchy, we collide into a crowd of two thousand locals, one of whom dashes from the mob and slashes the neck of an English supporter standing on the other side of the street, 30 metres away from me. A crumpled-up body folds into the gutter. His hands grasp his neck. He cradles his wound. I am completely out of my depth, but manage to go over to the gutter and place my hand on his shoulder. Before I can say anything comforting, the riot police stampede round the bend and encircle the mêlée. I expected to be a spectator only, but human emotion is more palpable than any journalistic imperative when you see someone being stabbed.

I explain what I saw. They ask if I can identify anyone. No, I tell them. Too dark. Too quick. Too shocked. I hear the siren of the ambulance and cross the road to where my colleagues are standing. The gendarmes have no further use for me. 'We've got to get out of here,' I say.

We run into the nearest hotel. There are no rooms available, we are told, but they do offer us some temporary shelter. The waves of violence continue to lap across the city and up to the door of the hotel. We are dressed as hooligans and it's clear we're not very welcome in first-class company. After a few hours and a few drinks we are asked to leave. Despite several pleas, they tell us there is still no room for us. I try one last-ditch attempt. 'We are from the BBC.'

'Oh,' the receptionist says, 'we have some rooms booked for the BBC, but they haven't taken them up yet.'

In a dash for cover – and the duvet (I am shattered) – I claim them, not knowing whether Des Lynam would turn up later to kick us out of bed. Paul christens my room 'The Des Lynam Suite'. (No one claimed them, but I later discovered they were booked for Radio 1. To think I could have called my room 'The Zoë Ball Suite'. An altogether more appealing prospect.)

15th June 1998

It is hot on the day England are to play Tunisia. And it is 'hot' on the streets. From 11a.m. supporters are getting tanked up in pavement cafés.

I feel I have been here before or else I have seen *The French Connection* once too often. The side street of the Old Port looks dangerously inviting, especially if you are on the trawl for tickets. A Tunisian dressed in colourful African dress conspiratorially mouths, 'English – you want ticket?' At last a chance to see if I can pull off a street deal – and achieve just a little bit of what is required to pass myself off as a hooligan in this world. We haggle. The spit-and-sawdust deal gets me my Willie Wonka's golden match tickets for £60 each.

Puffed up by what I think is a terrific deal (they were selling at £200 a pop in Paris), I swagger back to the Old Port and join the mass of England fans. Paul says that violence seems inevitable. There is a scent of aggression among many of the England fans, he says – the language, the tempo and the temperature all point to the inevitable. I am not certain. When we arrive for the game outside the stadium, both sets of supporters attack each other. Again, I didn't anticipate the onset of hostilities. I have no feel for the situation. A brick narrowly misses my head. More madness, rioting and street fighting. I cower behind Paul. We eventually make it into the ground.

In the stadium I realize that it is perhaps not the wisest thing to have bought tickets for the wrong end. Paul and I spend most of the match in the Tunisian section covered by an expansive Tunisian flag. I'm not operating well in this world. Not well at all. With no hesitation, Paul admits he's having doubts, too. He is being realistic and he's right. It's just one step to far.

We return to 'The Des Lynam Suite' to nurse our egos.

England 2 Tunisia 0

16th June 1998

Time to catch the train home. There were some sun-burned, tattooed, flush-cheeked lunatics on board getting drunk, being sick and yelling, 'Engerland, Engerland'. I keep my head down. After my tepid exploits my spirits are low. I can't see how we can possibly pull off this assignment. If I've got any sense, I'll bow out now. And then, just as I'm plotting to abandon ship on this one, I hear a couple of fans go at it full pelt, abusing every racial minority, the ticket inspector and even the beautiful game itself. They burst into raucous song:

> Wherever they go, we'll follow our team,
> For we are the Chelsea and we are supreme.

> We'll never be mastered by no northern bastards,
> And we'll keep the blue flag flying.

I've found some Chelsea fans at last, but whether they're Head-hunters or not is anyone's guess. They all terrify me – and the chants keep me company all the way home.

> Celery, celery,
> If she don't come,
> I'll tickle her bum,
> With a lump of celery.

There is as wide a gulf between their bumptious mood and my low spirits as there is between who I am and the person I am trying to become. I may not be able to close that gap. For the moment, I smoke a cigarette for effect – to look busy, to distract me from my own fears and insecurities. I don't really smoke. At least not yet. I have never smoked, but I have found that if you are wearing covert equipment and you don't want people to be too tactile then smoking is the perfect defence because you can just move your lit cigarette towards anyone who is getting too close. (In fact smoking, like drinking, has always been a problem in my undercover work. After the *World In Action* programme featuring me as an undercover bouncer was transmitted, viewers phoned in with two predominant sentiments: 'He smokes like a sixteen-year-old girl', and 'He smokes like he doesn't inhale'.)

17th June 1998

Time for a council of war in the BBC offices in London. I do not air the negativity I felt yesterday. Instead, I mumble assurances. 'We're doing well. It's only a matter of time... we just need to assimilate...

we're out of our depth but I'm sure we'll manage it.' I don't think for one second that Alex believes me. Alex knows me and knows that I'm reluctant to give up on challenges, even if they become too much for me. So suspicious is he of my rose-tinted perspective that he threatens to accompany us on our next foray into football. Time for a double espresso. Or two?

18th June 1998

While I am recovering from football, Alex is talking to investigative journalist Lisa Brinkworth about a story that she has been researching for over a year. She has taken it to other production companies, but none of the networks thinks it is a story that is obtainable, or indeed one that is relevant. The task is to enter a foreign country and expose the sordid side of the most alluring and glamorous industry in the world. The task is to infiltrate a specific gang of PRs, or 'Moonsinners' as they call themselves, find out how they operate and reveal their links with the rest of the fashion industry. Alex decides to send Lisa and producer Colin Barr to Milan to see if it is one for us.

25th June 1998

The BBC now has a team van travelling to the World Cup. There are six of us, including Paul, who's now had his head shaved to look the part, and me. (I vowed never to have my head shaved after going undercover as a bouncer in Nottingham for eleven months.) It's a full complement. Everyone else is relieved not to have to run the gauntlet of vomit-spattered trains and pissed-up fans. For me, though, I could probably have done with the practice that such train journeys afford me. After all, I've got to learn to be a thug, not a tourist.

We have decided that the Romanian game would not particularly aid me in assimilation and would not be a focus for violence because the Romanians do not a have a travelling firm of hooligans like the English. We've also heard from a reliable contact that some of the

Chelsea Head-hunters are on their way to England's remaining Group-G match against Columbia in Lens. That's why we're here.

Alex has carried out his threat and accompanies us to make sure we're not investing time and money in a project that could be an expensive – or fatal – flop. These expeditions don't just pose physical risks but also financial ones. The BBC know that, for all their investment, these are fragile projects and through no fault of our own we may produce nothing – we may be found out and we may be compromised. That's the other risk we have to take.

This time we have covert equipment on board. We want to film them. There are 30,000 English fans here and finding a Head-hunter will be difficult – filming them could be even harder. We are hoping for a chance sighting, but the odds are against us in this sea of people and football frenzy. The police couldn't find them at the ports to prevent them from arriving in France – what hope have we of finding them here?

We are staying in Lille, a few miles away from Lens, where the game is taking place. Police sirens reverberated through the streets all last night. It's like watching an American police movie. Just when your eye tires of one drama, another one unfolds in front of you. From corner to corner, crowds of fans run and splinter and fight – run and converge to fight the police and some of the local French gangs. Bottles and missiles and everything that isn't tied down become weapons. Clearly the England fans are making their presence felt. They start drinking from 10.30a.m. and don't stop. The locals hate the English because they have brought riots to their streets. They despise the lager louts and have had enough. No wonder some of their number fight back. A number of local malcontents, however, use the England fans as an excuse to create mayhem too.

26th June 1998

It's the day of the game. For our part we are still hunting down the Head-hunters. Bars and cafés being the safest bet, Paul and I head off to scour Lens while Alex and Lee, our researcher, stay in Lille. We're all togged up with wires and hidden bag cameras, which is just as well as Alex and Lee get lucky. They find the Chelsea Head-hunters openly snorting cocaine off a table in a bar and sit down at a table next to them pretending to be drunken fans. No one seems to object to their flagrant drug use. Alex and Lee identify them from the Own Goal trial photographs, and film them secretly until the tape runs out. For all the European border controls and police checks, the Head-hunters have made it to the World Cup – the greatest sporting stage on earth. This is the break I've been hoping for. I view the tape in the hotel at night. I watch to learn what I have to become. I know I have no chance of impersonating these hooligans, but that's not what I tell the others. We must stay positive.

While the team celebrates that success, Paul and I are under pressure in Lens, a couple of hours before the game. Despite the alcohol ban, there are drunken fans everywhere. Chewing baguettes, we come to rest on a grassy slope, where nearly 5,000 fans are gathered. Every inch of space is covered with English paraphernalia and punctuated with bottles of beer. We find a spot to one side. The gendarmes maintain a significant presence. Slowly, as the day heats up, I detect a red mist rising. It is going to kick off as they say when violence is about to explode. The crowd on the bank seem to assume battle stations. Eruption seems imminent. Paul senses it, too. 'Come on, Donal, it's not safe.'

We walk away slowly, calmly, trying not to betray our sweaty terrors. A bottle cracks on the tarmac behind me, first one and then lots. Sirens begin screaming from every direction. We retreat to a back street close to the train station. They're at it again. I think I've had enough of assimilation for one day.

Tough. This is work and there's no respite. While thousands are enjoying the game, we are on the trail of some elusive cocaine-snorting fans. On the corner of one long boulevard, outside a pub, I see someone I recognize instantly from the mug-shots. It is Stuart Glass. He is a leader. He illuminates and animates conversation. His jokes are the funniest, or else his company think it's better to laugh harder at his humour than anyone else's. I watch him and his gang interact, and realize he's unique. When he moves, so do his troops; when he shouts, they shout. His gang look to him for a lead in anything they do – I'd swear they'd only go to the toilet with his blessing. His every move is deliberate, every tick planned and every toss of the head choreographed for effect. I can learn a lot from him.

Their leader demands lager and drugs and they are busy servicing his needs. One of his acolytes asks us if we can get him cocaine. We disappoint. Glass was a National Front candidate for the council elections in the 1970s. He achieved notoriety among the NF faithful when he won the annual NF Yard of Ale competition.

Right now, Glass is wearing reflective silver shades. He never takes them off. He never meets anyone's gaze unless he has to. It's all in the eyes – the suspicion, the strength, the fear. It's going to be very difficult to penetrate this man's domain, particularly when I can't read his mind, can't see his eyes.

It is my first face-to-face exchange with them, and I'm in trouble. Perspiration is pouring out of places that only I can sense. Luckily, the interaction doesn't last long enough for it to spill forth. I look the part, but barely survive the forty-five-second encounter. However, it is sufficient. They consider me viable enough in their world to be a conduit for drugs. At least that is a good sign.

We keep an eye on them from a distance. They leave the street café. It is a considered move. They meet the riot police, who remain unmoved. Faced with a wall of shields, they retreat and, despite my best attempts at following Glass in the crowd, I lose him.

29th June 1998

We are at St Etienne, relaxing before the England game tomorrow. The entire town square is taken up by a giant screen which is relaying today's match – Germany vs Mexico – live. For once, there is no hint of violence. As we watch, the team and I munch baguettes filled with mayonnaise and chips, our staple diet here.

Suddenly, there is a tremor, a rumble in the crowd, a scuffle and then a stampede. Three thousand people take flight in a tiny space filled with beer tents, enclosed by a two-foot ledge and a flower bed. Fear takes flight very easily and I'm gone. I've got no idea why I am running, other than the fact that everyone else is. I vault over the ledge into the perimeter road and stop behind some cars. Paul and I regroup. We gulp for oxygen. Still in the aftermath of the bull run, no one seems to have any idea what ignited it. Ambulances arrive. The injured are taken to hospital. The team tries to link up, but one of our number is missing. It is Pip, the producer. We phone his mobile. He is in an ambulance.

The hospital treats casualties from the stampede, some walking wounded, one prostrate. Pip is prostrate. His knee is seriously damaged and they plaster it from ankle to hip. He tripped up on the ledge in the middle of the stampede. Still, he is in good spirits. We take him back to the hotel and lay him on a bed with his leg propped up on a mound of pillows. He will go home tomorrow by train, an injured soldier from the Battle of Wounded Knee.

30th June 1998

Today it's Argentina vs England. Crunch time. There are no tickets to be bought anywhere. Paul and I join the majority of English fans around the screen in the main square. The authorities, however, decide, to cancel the screening in the wake of yesterday's violence. For the thousands of ticketless supporters, there is nowhere to watch the game other than in a few bars and restaurants. There are some scuffles around the square, where distressed fans gather to drink. We get out safely and find a pub that's showing the game. The penalty shoot-out is a disaster. England lose. The aggression erupts with the end of the match. One Chelsea fan, associated with the Head-hunters, launches a call to arms: 'Come on, let's get them'.

Shards of glass lash past my face from the broken bottles that smash off the wall beside me. We are in the thick of battle again. I stand awkwardly to the back of this mob. It's a close call – if you're not with them, you're against them. They race down the street, punching and screaming at everyone in their path. Cars are smashed and shop windows broken with bricks. I decide enough's enough. However far back I drift from these rioters, I'm still vulnerable to arrest just for being in their company. Snatch squads of riot police are pulling fans and hooligans from the street. I pull back. It's the right decision – for now.

9th July 1998

England is out of the World Cup and we are back home in one piece – just. Alex is now convinced he's getting his money's worth. But, still, the question is asked: can Donal make it as a convincing thug? The answer is maybe. We agree it's worth a try, and so I get the go-ahead – the licence to be a football hooligan, to be a Head-hunter.

11th July 1998

In order to be a good hooligan I must first become a good Loyalist. I've got a Southern Irish accent which is anathema to most of the Chelsea hooligans, who have strong right-wing and neo-Nazi sympathies. Another appendage to their mixed bag of political beliefs is an attachment to the armed Loyalist cause in Northern Ireland. The team and I think the best way to explain my brogue is to reinvent myself as a violent Loyalist. It means I have to change both my politics and my accent. One is easier than the other. I may do a bit of play-acting from time to time but I am no impressionist.

Today is the Orange Order's biggest parade on the UK mainland, in Southport, Merseyside. It may be important for me later on to be able to say that I was here. To do so would earn me much kudos, but I have no idea when and how I can benefit from it; I just

43

know that I will. It is just one prop and one thread in a thousand that will help weave me into the hooligan I have to become to investigate this hideous mob.

The parade gets under way to cries of 'Fuck the Pope'. I buy the British National Party's newspaper, *Insignia*, and hold it throughout the day – another theatrical prop for my armoury. On the whole, the march is a colourful, family affair, but there are certainly a few on the lunatic fringe. I walk along and try to sing some of the songs. Everyone is swept along with the occasion and no one takes any notice of me. Why should they? My biggest task of the day is to buy some Loyalist music tapes. I'll have to learn the songs and keep them as unspoken testimony of who I am and what I stand for. I walk over to a stand and point to two cassettes. I try not to utter a word, so terrified am I that my distinctly Southern Irish accent will find me out. It's pitiful. Get a grip, Donal, I tell myself. In the end I just point at the tapes and they are handed over. No words are exchanged. There is a long way to go.

15th July 1998

After much talk in the office the team has decided that we should try and investigate the very dangerous and all-pervasive Nigerian 419 con men. From the research that we have pulled together we know that we are going to have to be very convincing to both entice and entrap the fraudsters – that is, when we find them. But before that we have to have a plan because we may have to act quickly when we do make contact.

We want to see the scam from the inside out, from the viewpoint of the victim and the perpetrator. How do we do that? Alex believes that the only way we can do it without breaking the law ourselves or being complicit in breaking the law, is to provide our own mark or victim and invite the Nigerian con men to defraud him for a share of the profits. I could approach the con men and say that I have a friend who has lots of money and say I want a share of the proceeds if they help me to separate my friend from his money. This may work. This is a plan in evolution. It will be ready by the time I get in contact with the con men – I hope.

17th July 1998

The fashion investigators Colin and Lisa leave London for Milan on a fashion fact-finding mission. The preliminary research that Lisa has done suggests a very strong and disturbing environment. This trip will decide if there is a story to be told and if we can tell it – penetrate it and expose it. On her previous journeys to Milan, Lisa met some of the PRs and they think that she is a fashion writer and ex-model. They believe she is one of their own – safe, a co-conspirator in the *omerta* that pervades this industry. Only insiders know and they won't tell.

20th July 1998

Victims once used newspapers and the courts for justice – now they use the Internet as well. I trawl cyberspace for some information about the Nigerian 419 fraud and it sprouts a range of pitiful tales about how the con men duped a multiplicity of victims. Some have been wiped out of their life savings and some marks have been manipulated into aiding and abetting the fraud of others. These 'magic money' hoaxes seemed to be the stuff of urban legends to me, but there is pain and hurt in the victims' accounts and it is real and palpable. I decide to focus on this extraordinary and devious ruse and to try and reveal it for what it is. How do I do that? I have no idea – yet.

23rd July 1998

The Milan fashion story proves to be as sordid as we expected.
Colin and Lisa arrive from their exploratory mission. I meet

Colin at Terminal 2 at Heathrow airport. He has seen the PRs in action – up close and all too personal. He tells me that one turned up at a model residency to collect some models for the clubs, but left very angry. The sin – one of the girls was wearing trousers instead of a skirt. Because he was in a hurry he didn't have time to send her back in to change. The PR, Oliver, took the girls (who were about sixteen) to the club and placed them at a table with two middle-aged businessmen. The young girls got bored and, like schoolchildren (they're barely out of school), started throwing peanuts about. Oliver dropped his trousers in front of the young models and waved his penis in their faces. Later, with his trousers pulled up, he jumped on them. They objected. They were bored and drunk and young. Colin and Lisa witnessed this scene and recoiled.

Over the next few months we will develop a strategy to enter this world and reveal it from the inside out.

26th July 1998

I don't have much time to have a holiday this year, probably just a few days here and there. Except for one week – one special week that I reserved six months ago. It is a mission to the outback. This is not undercover. This is not work. This is pleasure – sheer indulgence. It is my time. My holiday – my adventure. It's a 6,000-mile flight for a 133-km canoe race through jungle and wild, dangerous and inviting rapids. Above all, canoeing is my passion. Time to bring the test card down on my life as a television reporter. For the next week or so, I am simply me.

27th July 1998

I arrive. It is hot, unbelievably so. Television lights are staring down on me. I leave London as a reporter and travel across the globe to be reported on. It is strange being on the other side of media street. It seems I can't get away from television – not even on holiday.

1st August 1998

Panic is not always palpable. Now there is no disguising it. Panic is often an athlete's best friend. It gets the adrenaline going and gets you in the 'zone'. Today it makes me want to go to the toilet all the time.

The river is low, but I am flowing. The crowds are gathering at the start. There are TV helicopters flying overhead. The rescue services are nearby. There have been fatalities in the race before and they are very safety-conscious.

We lead from the gun and race to the first weir. It is bone dry. We climb over it with crews bashing and crashing into us. We stumble back further as the dry heat makes us flag, but eventually finish four hours and twenty minutes later in fourth place with a day to go.

I am so tired I fall out of the boat and crawl to the bank covered in mud. Two bodies extend their arms and lift me to my feet. There is relief and pain and shock.

2nd August 1998

There is carnage on the course. The rescue helicopters hover over the valley, where access by air is the only option in an emergency. We didn't have an emergency, but we had a few disasters. We moved up to second place at one stage because of mishaps that crippled other boats, but we come a cropper ourselves and eventually finish eighth overall after nearly seven hours of racing today.

Seconds out of the water and a microphone is thrust into my face. I feel like the oldest athlete in the world: drawn, lined, fatigued – and flat on my feet. Still, I talk the talk and deliver the sound bite the journalists want. It's time for home.

6th August 1998

I didn't take Stop 'n' Grow out to Australia with me, and my almost stress-free trip has actually given me something to cut, groove and manicure. But I don't have a pair of scissors to hand – so I begin to nibble them into shape and that is that: my road to recovery has been thwarted. I keep nibbling and soon my manicure turns into a massacre. That can only mean one thing: football is around the corner.

10th August 1998

Today we have to choreograph the con man's dance. I have to prepare a strategy to entice our 419 fraudsters and to cast our spell on them. I need to provide them with a pot of gold and a means to steal it. Alex is thinking big. He suggests that I should be the bodyguard to a lottery winner. A disgruntled bodyguard who is anxious to help relieve his boss of his new-found wealth. I've been a bouncer before, so a bodyguard shouldn't be too difficult. However, where are we going to find a lottery winner? We'll invent one. We'll lay the seeds over the next few weeks and see just what sprouts.

13th August 1998

While I was away, Pip (now out of plaster) did some routine journalistic phone-bashing, calling people in the care profession to discover if there is an industry-wide concern about standards. It turns out there is – so much so that the Government is considering setting up independent inspection procedures. But just what should the standards be? And just how bad are the current practices? These are the questions that need addressing. Neither can be answered fully by me unless I work at a care home. The feedback from the care professionals suggests that this story is relevant and important.

15th August 1998

A friend spoke to a bomber today. The bomber killed twenty-nine people and injured 370. My friend forwarded the warning from the bomber to the Royal Ulster Constabulary, along agreed guidelines that all public bodies have to hand for such events. Another call is received elsewhere. Another warning is delivered.

The news comes across the radio. A bombing in Omagh in Northern Ireland. First five, then ten and finally twenty-eight bodies are catalogued (another victim died later in hospital). An ordinary afternoon in a quiet market town is destroyed as people are indiscriminately blown to pieces. The dead and wounded come from both communities in more or less equal proportion.

Just as my adventure as a journalist gathers momentum, my brother and his wife today begin their life outside journalism. They are moving to the Republic to run a pub in an idyllic part of the country. They had both been working in television news. Today, they leave their reporting lives behind to start a new life away from the violence in Northern Ireland. They represent both traditions in Northern Ireland, but have reported on too many funerals and covered too many bombings to want to report and live there any longer.

My brother and his wife are an hour into the journey south when they hear the news. Not ring-fenced by their reporting roles on this day, they pull over, hug their children and cry together. Today they are simply ordinary parents – civilians – with nothing to separate them from the inhumanity of this awful deed.

Only later do they hear that it was a very close friend who took the warning call, who talked to the bomber, who spoke to the person who took twenty-nine lives. Nobody ever thinks about the trauma of taking those calls, do they? I certainly never did. I did some work today, but it hardly matters – how can it?

It is strange that as my family tries to divest itself of Ireland's past, I am trying to steal it to play my role as an extreme Loyalist-supporting, far right football hooligan.

16th August 1998

We are trying to find Jason Marriner, long-time Chelsea Head-hunter and our target. We chose him because he had escaped jail

and convictions for football violence, despite being a major organizer for many years. We'd heard that he was affable and liked to
tell a good story. We thought that that might help, seeing that we,
too, are story-tellers. He, for the moment, is our number-one target.

No question what was on his mind when he bought his home:
Chelsea Close. To try and get close to this man we start to drink
in his two locals – discovered after numerous scouting missions –
and work on creating an impression on him and his retinue. We
have our own entourage – a five-strong stakeout team. First,
though, we have to decide how to enter his domain. Should I go in
weak or strong? This is where undercover journalism mutates
into a blend of intricate streetwise craft and Freudian psychology.
If I enter Jason's world in a subordinate role, as someone who
looks up to him, I won't be sufficiently interesting for him to want
to know.

We turn over every permutation, twist and multiplier-effect for
various routes into Jason's life, and it's decided we go in strong. We
have to measure the effect of our every move with Jason and weigh
up the results that it will serve up in nine or twelve months' time.
What will make him suspicious? What will entice him, and what
will make him want to be my friend?

We remember the World Cup, Stuart Glass's little cocaine side-
show. Could this be something Jason might go for? A drug dealer?
The team thinks it's a goer, and so I'm cast. A drug dealer. That's me.

First impressions count. To create the image, I adopt the props
of a typical drug dealer: the shades, Puffa jacket (even in summer),
baseball cap, at least one mobile phone and an expensive, flashy-
looking car (a Merc). I top it all by carrying wads of ready money.
An instant transformation and it works. People glance once and
turn away quickly – must be a drug dealer.

Since I've come back from Australia, Paul and I have been cruis-
ing Hampton Hill in the silver Merc, techno music blaring from the
open windows, anxious to be seen and heard. People notice us all
right. They read the signs and keep out of our way. Everywhere we

go, we see fear on their faces and know our props are working. But now they must work with Jason.

Then, today, we get our chance. Jason has been spotted in the garden of the Clarence pub, just off Hampton High Street. A BBC couple doing a stakeout for us phone me discreetly and tell me where our man is. Paul and I race into action with the car and the music. We swagger into the pub ostentatiously.

There is no doubting that he's personally registered our arrival but he is keen not to show it. He was not going to lend me any credibility until he knows a little bit more about the new arrival on his patch.

This is not the first time I have seen him. But it is the first time at close quarters. He is smaller, stockier, louder and more lively company than I had previously imagined. Both legs are almost covered Yakuza-like in distinctive tattoos. One on the back of his leg told his life story:

'When we're good, they never remember
When we're bad, they never forget'.

He is leading his friends in a cacophony of obscenities. He is talking 'large' about some fight he was involved in. Snippets of conversation drift over to the other tables in the beer garden. He then starts bragging about his conquests.

'I was shagging this bird. She was a babe but she had the painters in if you know what I mean!' he laughs.

He shows no sign of having noticed us, although I take this to be deliberate. It's his manor – this is his terrain. Jason is playing cool.

After making the best of my moments on the phone, I get up to leave. My eyes catch his. He's playing strong, the hard man in town, refusing to be intimidated. I blurt out, 'Alwight, mate?' to him. He ignores me. As soon as I've done it, I know I've made a monumental gaff. Paul knows it too, but he doesn't say.

We walk out of the bar and I know I have undone a lot of good work. The goal is to get *Jason* to make the big approach, to make him so curious about me that he can't resist approaching to find out more. That would put me in a position of strength and would also remove any sense that he was being courted by me in the way that undercover police would work.

He, after all, is a member of a gang that was infiltrated by police just a decade or so ago for the infamous Own Goal trials. I tell the rest of the team that I've become aware that I am harder on everyone else's mistakes than I am on my own. 'For that I apologize,' I say. They all laugh.

I have made a mistake. I promise myself that I can recover. If I don't, I will have to shoulder responsibility for the disaster. Little mistakes can have serious consequences.

17th August 1998

Today Jason is under surveillance. We know where he lives and the pubs he drinks in, but we don't know where he works. I need to know his pattern of behaviour, his haunts, his movements and idiosyncrasies. However, tracking him is proving harder than expected.

Our team is not trained in surveillance and we only have limited numbers. Neither Paul nor I can be used as it would compromise our roles in the coming months if we were spotted, so Alex and Pip are drafted in. Pip is keeping a look-out from a black van outside Jason's house to catch his early-morning routine, while Alex waits in his car on Hampton High Street, preparing to follow Jason if he leaves in his car.

I am in contact with the team by phone, available for a walk-on part if they locate Jason in a public place. Accidental collisions are crucial. I don't intend to speak to him, I just want him to see me, to get a sense of who I am and what I am about. I want him to pick up on our clues, to trade on his intuition and to value me as someone to know. He will be adding up all the semaphores, the hints and the footprints we've left behind, but he won't know that I am inventing them for his benefit alone.

It is a long wait for Pip in the van. Jason is having a lie-in. It is gone 10.30a.m. when he eventually leaves Chelsea Close flats and goes to a café nearby, where he attacks a bacon butty. Alex tails him at a distance to a couple of businesses, but neither turns out to be Jason's workplace. It is frustrating. The football season is about to start and we have limited information on our chubby friend. We do know he is a major organizer of violence, that he is dangerous and very wary. That's the big picture, but it's the fine detail we're after – Jason's habits, how he thinks, how he operates. On that front, progress is slow.

18th August 1998

Furtive attempts are being made to approach a man whom we believe runs the Nigerian 'magic money' scam in London. His name is Solomon. He is the mastermind of the London end of a world-wide scam. I send a message through a contact to say that there is mutual benefit in meeting up. It says that I have a lottery winner in my sights and that he could also be in Solomon's sights, if he so wishes. The message is passed on. I wait.

Later, contact is made and a meeting is to be arranged at my convenience. As a bodyguard living with my Northern-based lottery winner, I suggest a get-together in Manchester. Solomon agrees. We dreamt this story and I've been researching my role by reading Andy McNab and buying gun magazines. When this year is over, if I need a bodyguard, at least I'll know what to look for!

20th August 1998

The early-morning surveillance outside Jason's continues. Today a 'For Rent' sign is sighted outside Chelsea Close before Jason rises. Pip phones me with delight in his voice. 'How would you like to be Jason's neighbour?'

Moving in upstairs to a football hooligan isn't everyone's

favourite real-estate option, but for the moment it's my idea of heaven. I ring up the estate agency and arrange a viewing. This could be the breakthrough we've been looking for.

21st August 1998

There are a couple of constants in Jason's life. There is football. That is number one. There is food and then there is more food. In Hampton Hill, around pub closing time, it is a good bet that the our man will be seen rubbing his belly, hungry for a bit of ethnic cuisine. For such a racist I have always wondered why he condescends to foreign food. It doesn't make sense and why would it? Racism is a nonsensical standpoint and I can't begin to make sense of it.

If there is one place we know where we can find him after hundreds of hours on his trail, it is in the local Chinese restaurant. In here he heaps the same abuse and the same jokes about squinty eyes at the owner that he has done for as long as he has been going there. For as long as he is in there, it is his domain. He commands attention and leads the conversation. I get a report this evening from our spotter Lee that Jason is at the Chinese and I amble up to join the queue.

I find Jason with an odd collection of people, all obviously known to him, including 'Rangers Man' (as I decide to dub him) and another local. Rangers Man (supporter of Glasgow Rangers, a Protestant-affiliated team) is drunkenly berating the local for reading the Lifestyle section of his newspaper and not the story about the Omagh bomb – it is six days since that terrible incident and the papers are running pictures of the funerals of some of the victims. It is getting very heated.

'Ye can't stand by while your brethren are being mowed down. Look at our brethren – should be worried about them and not about your food, mate,' he says. He leaves in disgust, clutching his curried chips and fried rice in zealous embrace.

'Ah,' I say to myself, 'this is what they call a window of opportunity.' In fact my opportunity is walking out the door. 'He's right mate – you know he's right.' I let the whole restaurant know as I walk out to share my views with Rangers Man. Mindful of Jason's association with extreme Loyalists I am sure that he has caught the significance of my comments. As the Greek chorus in the Chinese (if there can be a Greek chorus in a Chinese) Jason is almost obliged to report on the dramatic events unfolding in front of him. He duly obliges.

'Once a Protestant, always a Protestant, you just can't help yourself,' he says to his hungry ensemble. He's made the association. In his mind I am now a Northern Irish Protestant, therefore a Loyalist and sympathetic to his own political views. It is one step closer into Jason's head and one more pit stop to his inner circle.

He is a very careful man; his football friends have been with him for nearly fifteen years. To try and get close to him will be difficult, but today is one more step on the ladder. In many ways my break and my opportunity acts as a sticking plaster on my earlier near-fatal blunder when I blurted out an inappropriate salutation to the Hampton Head-hunter. I am playing ball again.

22nd August 1998

It's the first home game of the season: Chelsea vs Newcastle United. My football hooligan kit sits very uncomfortably on me. The shades I can just about handle, but the white Reebok classics are complete anathema to me. 'It's got to be done, if you want to do the job, Donal,' Paul insists. He is in similar garb. I wince and reluctantly lace up the awful trainers.

Ticket touts line the Fulham Road. I pick one out and ask him for two together or 'a carpet'. They cost £50 each. We exchange money and tickets and join the throngs walking to the game. There is a large police presence. This is my first time game at Stamford Bridge. With so much going on, it's hard to concentrate on my mission: to become a Chelsea supporter and to become one quickly. Kids, parents and hooligans – all chatting excitedly, buying programmes or eating hot dogs. I am drinking coffee – my standby in times of stress.

We walk into the west stand. The chanting begins. I listen intently, trying to decipher every word and syllable, like a teenager desperately drawing meaning out of every word of a pop song. 'One man went to mow, went to mow a meadow...' No amount of research from videos and books can ever make up for this, my on-the-spot Chelsea tutorial.

'... Four men went to mow, went to mow a meadow, four men, three men, two men, one man and his dog, went to mow a meadow.'

The ground has a cathedral-like atmosphere and every chant has a life of its own. Only the person who starts the chant knows where it came from. There are many false dawns, chants that are only ever sung by one or two or ten fans and then die when they fail to achieve momentum. Why some are kick-started by one and then sung by 40,000 while some fail to evolve is a mystery to me.

There is no threat of exposure here. There is only my wide-eyed excitement at the crowd, the intimacy of the pitch and players and the realization that this is what it is all about. Twenty-two men and a ball. I suppose if it wasn't football something else would bring the hooligan out of the hooligan.

'Ten men went to mow, went to mow a meadow. Ten men, nine men, eight men, seven men, six men, five men, four men, three men, two men, one man AND HIS DOG SPOT went to mow a meadow. CHELSEA CHELSEA CHELSEA CHELSEA.'

Fortunately, this chant is one I can join in on without much fear of exposing my thin relationship with the club.

Jason is almost certainly here – I can sense it – but I don't know where. Unbelievably, he has a season ticket. Most of his friends are denied that privilege because they are banned from all football grounds. Many of them still sneak into matches but there are serious consequences if they are caught. Jason, whose name is certainly known to the police, does not have a conviction for football violence and can therefore buy a season ticket. It is a testament to his cunning that he has not yet been caught, despite being a major force for violence over the last fifteen years at home and abroad.

'... And we don't give a fuck whoever you may be, because we are the famous CFC,' the Chelsea Cathedral Choir roars to the tune of 'Lord of the Dance'. The game ends in a 1–1 draw.

Jason leaves and gets into his purple Renault car. For a while Alex and Pip follow him. I get a call back in a café near the ground.

'I think he has clocked us following him,' Pip says.

Alex pauses and then says, 'No, I think he's just looking at the car because it is a distinctive green.'

Next time, we'll hire a more unobtrusive car for surveillance. I head for Hampton to walk into Jason's life again. He doesn't come out to play. Still, some of his friends have seen me and the point is made. It is infiltration by association. Another inch closer.

24th August 1998

There is progress on the care story. Pip has contacted me to tell me that after hundreds of conversations and calls to people in the industry, he has identified a number of care homes for a visit or at least a job application. They all seem to have inadequate training for staff and poor service for clients. Some of the allegations are more serious. This is a sensitive and delicate story and we are going to spend a lot of time discussing just which home I should investigate closely.

26th August 1998

Colin and Lisa and I talk about my entrée into fashion. We roll over and filter several roles for me in that industry, but we need one that allows me to jump up and down the social scale where appropriate. They suggest playing a photographer – I'm looking scruffy and unkempt and look the part without trying. I don't have to be a good photographer, just look like one. Lisa and Colin will create a history for me in fashion as a photographer and tell a couple of the main characters in Milan about me to make it easier for me to hit the ground running. The first focus will be two PRs, one called Oliver and the other called Diego. They are members of the Moonsinners. There is not much time to get it right in fashion. It is all about the London–Milan–Paris circuit, a turbulent three-week spell when the new collections are shown. Progress must be quick. The shows start at the end of September.

27th August 1998

My phone rings in the early hours. My mom is seriously ill. She lost the sight in one eye some years ago when caustic soda splashed into her eye. Today the doctors are trying to save her only working eye. Her eye pressure is 39. The normal is 10. If it goes to 60, she will lose her sight. I fly out of Heathrow on the first available flight to see her in a Dublin hospital. It is a glorious day, but it's grey and fuzzy to my mom. She can see my outline and embraces it – embraces me. As ever, she is entertaining those around her and is very positive. She is in good hands. Notwithstanding that, we are all worried.

28th August 1998

I visit Mom again today. Her eye pressure is down but her vision is still grey. She is optimistic, but I can see an underlying terror at the prospect of learning Braille at 63 years of age. Doctors have suggested this to her in the past when she had her original eye problems. She didn't listen to them then and she won't now. I fly out to London on an evening flight.

1st September 1998

Jason has a new neighbour. I pick up the key for my new home in Chelsea Close, just one floor up from Jason's flat. If we exploit this situation right, he won't be able to ignore me. After all, it's a small block of flats and my door is just 25 metres from his.

It's a small, sparse flat with one bedroom and a small lounge and kitchen. There's enough room for a sofa and a big telly, which is all that I need – well, that and an armoury of surveillance equipment. Hopefully, I'll get Jason to visit. I scour the flat for secret camera positions and spot a few possibilities. I add 'stereo' to my shopping list. They're always an easy option because you can put a microphone in the speakers. If someone asks you to play it, you just say it's broken.

We have our very own 'Q' figure who provides me with my covert equipment. Like the Bond character, he is avuncular and protective and advises me on more than just equipment. He always leaves me with that *Hill Street Blues* line, 'Let's be careful out there'.

2nd September 1998

We want Jason to see me move in. A black leather sofa is on standby in a hired Thrifty van and the plan is to move the furniture when Jason leaves the flat. Pip is in another van across the road with a camera to film proceedings. Unfortunately, Jason surprises us all and leaves at 8.30a.m. while Pip is still setting up his equipment. We miss our cue. I don't know whether to feel sorry or not. I'm wired for sound, but not wearing a camera. I'm too nervous for that. It's important to be comfortable physically and psychologically when wearing the kit, otherwise it's difficult to perform well undercover. It's best to wear the heavy and full complement of kit only when absolutely necessary. The recorder is strapped onto my back and the rest of the technical equipment is tucked in and around my torso. I have to wear one extra layer over my tee-shirt to disguise the bulk of the equipment. I have to be careful about my weight, because any extra pounds can make it difficult to conceal the covert equipment – and, even, to wear it. It's a careful balance between this and my diet as a lager lout.

3rd September 1998

I arrive in Manchester to case the city for a location to meet our 419 gang. The site must be visible from the road, where a covert film unit can catch them on a long lens. We think we've found it.

The full team is ready to greet Solomon in Manchester. We have chosen a restaurant with open-window frontage to allow us to get perfect camera angles from the street. I am wearing a radio microphone, which is being picked up by the soundman in a van outside. Dressed immaculately in a suit and with slicked-back hair, I am Mac, with a soldier's temperament, strict on punctuality and strong of purpose. I have rehearsed my lines from a prepared script that the team and I have worked out to entice our con man.

The two tables opposite mine are full of BBC personnel today, all at the ready, awaiting Solomon's arrival. One table has a handbag facing my table and another has a briefcase trained in my direction. There are eight people playing walk-on parts for the BBC in this elaborate set-up. We are all dressed up, but there can be no party if Solomon doesn't show. We receive a call from the man himself. He says he'll try and make it. Two hours later we decide to blow him out so that our hand remains strong. We don't like to be kept waiting, we tell him. Solomon says there is a mark in London who is proving reluctant and the situation requires his attention. He apologizes and promises to rearrange shortly. We are hugely disappointed. We have invested a lot of time and effort for this no-show. One step forward, two steps back.

After an initial operation, my mother's eye pressure is back up to dangerous levels. Another operation is planned. I've been on the phone to her and she is cheering me up and telling me not to worry.

4th September 1998

This time we are prepared. I am determined that Jason will see me move in with the black sofa. Paul and I are set for a repeat performance.

The strategy not just engages what he is thinking, but also what he thinks I am thinking and how that manifests itself back into his thought processes. It's an intricate and intimate matrix.

Sometimes it becomes too intricate and we begin to overintellectualize the process, this psychological warfare. For the moment, the strategy is running along straight lines and the sofa is our simple and effective tool. It is waiting in the Thrifty van with the doors open. Paul and I are in the flat, poised to scoot down the stairs and retrieve said sofa as soon as Jason leaves.

Finally, Jason moves. We swing into action. As he walks towards his car, Paul and I start manhandling the sofa out of the van, heaving and puffing for theatrical effect. I can't see Jason, but I hear the door of his car slam. His eyeline is straight at me. I know he is watching me. I can feel it. I also know that, whatever I do, I must not catch him looking at me. That would make him feel uncomfortable. It would embarrass him and weaken my position. Rarely has a such a cheap sofa been moved with such import.

Jason starts the engine. I know he is still looking. Initially I have my back to him, but then I walk backwards, holding my end of the sofa up so I am sideways to him. Still no eye contact. His car isn't moving though. Just as I push open the swing doors to the block of flats Jason drives past. He has got the message: the boys are moving in.

5th September 1998

I fly to Dublin to see my mom. Her eye pressure is down to 15 after another minor operation. Her sight is improving. She can now read the headlines in a newspaper. It's a huge relief. I return to London on an evening flight.

6th September 1998

The Nigerian con men have been in contact. One of my colleagues, who has made himself available to me in my bodyguard role as a conduit for information, calls to say that they are interested in a meeting in London. They want to 'share information on how we can best take advantage of the situation that has presented itself' – their words. They are being cautious in expression and manner, as they always are. This may be why Solomon cried off before. Still, the hunt is on. We must be very careful not to scare away this quarry. They are, after all, the masters when it comes to deception. They have their lies – we have ours.

The sun shines on the Thames Valley and it is a glorious evening. The wooden benches outside the Clarence Pub are packed and again Jason is wearing his shorts. Lee, a young researcher, sits opposite him and his pals. Once again, as he has done many times before, he gets on the phone to me and discretely maps out the situation. 'Our man is outside. He is in company and it might well be worth a drive past or a quick drink if you want to make an impression,' he says.

'Give me five minutes, Lee,' I reply.

Paul and I slip on our shades and get into the rented Mercedes, assuming our drug-dealer personas. We drive down Hampton Hill High Street, windows down, music blaring, and park 40 metres past the pub, in full view of the packed beer garden. A glance in the rear-view mirror tells me that Jason is looking. His companions, too, draw their heads in my direction. Our charade works on ordinary members of the public, I know that, but it will have to be even more convincing to nail the Head-hunters. We mustn't slip up now. I remind myself to be cool, walk slowly, appear unfazed, the way gangsters do. In short, be everything I am not.

It's a very short walk to the pub. We pace it slow and measured. It's so ridiculously languid it's nearly a moon walk. I let my gaze drift up from the pavement as we approach. Jason is leaning on a pub bench, looking at me. I plan to pass him without remark but, unexpectedly, he leans further forward and deliberately catches my eye, holding the contact for longer than politeness allows. I swallow my excitement. 'Alwight, mate, alwight,' he says, taking the initiative. We respond in kind. His salutation informs everybody that he knows the new boys and that we are deserving of his respect.

We are in. After three solid months, Jason has said hello to me – on my terms. It's a huge relief. Despite living most of the last three years undercover in some form or capacity, I haven't quite got used to the time it takes to make even the very smallest of impressions.

7th September 1998

The flat is the perfect spy bunker. From my windows I can see all the movements in the Close. Equally, it means others can see in, so I am on the alert for prying neighbours. There is a huge amount of electronic circuitry in here and it wouldn't do to be seen wiring the camera in the washing machine to the recorder in the bedroom, or the sound transmitter (disguised as a TV remote) to the receiver. Ironically, Neighbourhood Watch is my biggest enemy.

Today, I am driving a borrowed Porsche. It is ten years old and needs a bit of a check up. I recognize Jason walking towards the flat and rush down the stairs to meet him. I want to move his recognition a fraction further. If I request a simple favour of him and he delivers, then I can return to him and thank him and that gives me another reason to interact with him.

'Sorry, mate,' I say to him before he enters the flats. 'Got a bit of problem with the motor. You don't know anyone who can sort it out without ripping me off?'

'No problems, mate. My pal down the road will sort you out. Tell him you're a mate of Jay's.'

'Sweet, mate, I appreciate that. Nice meeting you, pal. Macca's the name, just moved in upstairs. Don't know the area, man.'

'No problems, mate.'

'Sweet, sweet.'

Introductions made and the dance begins at close quarters. It's a long seduction process, but it's a lot easier if Jason thinks he needs to get to know me and Paul more than we need to get to know him. There is a delicate balance here. He wants to be shown respect as 'the man' in his manor, but he also needs to know the new boys in the neighbourhood in order to protect his status.

Paul and I pop along to the garage and put the car in. The mention of Jason's name gets instant recognition and premium service. His name obviously counts for a lot.

Fractions and increments – two steps forward, one step back – what kind of journalism is this?

9th September 1998

Jason is distressed. He's effing and blinding so loudly his curses echo around Chelsea Close. 'You fucking cunt, don't do it, you bastard, bollocks. I can't fucking believe it.'

I watch, discreetly, from my window above. Jason is trying to stuff a massive suitcase in the boot of his car. The boot is having none of it. Every time he slams it shut, it yawns open again. The volume level of curses is increasing with each slam. He gets on the mobile and berates someone liberally for selling him a duff car. I decide it's time to put in an appearance.

'Anything I can help you with, mate?'

'Goin' on holidays, mate, and the boot won't close. I've got me mate coming along. He's gonna drive me and sort it out later, fuckin' cunt.'

'Anywhere nice, mate?'

'Yeah, Crete for two weeks.'

'Sweet.'

'You don't have a fag, mate, do you?' he asks.

The odd thing is that Jason doesn't smoke. I reflect on this as I go up to the flat to get cigarettes and pick up a little thank-you present for him.

'Oi, thanks for sorting me out with the car,' I say, returning. 'Your geezer mate sorted me out right proper.'

'Did you mention my name?' He takes the proffered cigarette and another for the journey.

'I did and he looked after me. Listen, take that for your trouble.' I give him a new tee-shirt that I had upstairs and say that I acquired it on the black market. 'It stood me in nothin' so it will stand you in nothin'. Take it for your hols.'

He accepts happily. The gift offers a mark of respect. The acceptance says it is mutual. The cartographer is at work. Your life is mapped out, Jason, and you don't know it – you can't know it – at least I hope not. Unless you are turning me over. Unlikely. Life is strange, but not that strange.

The thing is though – he doesn't smoke.

10th September 1998

Today I make another arrangement to meet our fraudster, Solomon. We talk on mobiles. He sounds nervous and is not keen to meet outside his natural terrain of hotels and public places in and around London. I realize we tried to force him too much with the Manchester set-up. The stuff about having trouble with a mark sounded and felt like an excuse, although it would never do to say so. Perhaps it was true; either way, a hotel in Heathrow is going to be eminently more suitable. It was his idea, so we'll run with it.

The deal is done and the meet is set up. Whether he will show this time is anyone's guess. Having been bumped once, I am preparing to be let down again. My curiosity about the man is keen. What is he like? How dangerous is he? How smart is he? My guess is very smart. He has to be to reel in the size of fish he lands. I am concerned that we may fall foul of his suspicious mind. Are we making it too easy for him? Has he smelled a rat? If he has, we'll find out tomorrow night.

I get my suit ready and polish my shoes and sort out the rest of my secret camera wardrobe for stinging the stingers. You can put a covert camera in anything these days. The technology has made them so small that even if you were told that there was a camera in a tee-shirt you would find it hard to recognize the pin-hole lens. You can, however, feel it. The skill is weaving it into the fabric or insert-ing into a briefcase or even washing machine. The colour cameras are more sophisticated, but do not operate well in low light. For those conditions we use the smaller black-and-white cameras, which can get some extraordinary shots – mostly by accident. These automatic-focus cameras constantly amaze us. We will need to put that dexterity to good use in fashion, where a lot of action will take place in dark nightclubs and bars.

11th September 1998

I am at a Heathrow hotel. Our Nigerian friends are late. I pace up and down. Once again, the team is in place: in the lobby there is a 'businessman' with an open briefcase concealing a pin-hole camera, while opposite me sit two women with a rather unfashionable but functional handbag, also containing a camera. All of these characters are covert operatives for the BBC. I have my own covert gadgets, too – both my mobile and my Filofax are actually radio microphones. The latter is so well disguised that I can leave it open and even write on it without exposing or interfering with the inner circuitry.

The plan is to enjoy a drink with Solomon and his sidekick in the lobby and then take them up to the business conference room where we will have a bit more privacy. Two rather dull vases con-taining highly sophisticated cameras have already been positioned in the room to film the meeting – *if* it takes place.

I am feeling apprehensive now. My left leg is shaking. There is tingling on the back of my neck. I have felt this at the start of canoe races, this hyped-up mixture of tension and adrenaline which readies you for fight or flight. I don't know what to expect from these guys.

A tall black man arrives. He is very well dressed and has a body-guard with him. The bodyguard is big and broad and menacing. I am a bodyguard today, but I am not quite as sullen as Solomon's bodyguard. Sullen or stoned. Could be both?

Drinks are exchanged and handshakes shared. Solomon has a

large brandy and I have a large Irish whiskey. I don't drink whiskey, but a bodyguard might. Visually, I screen Solomon for bulges in his breast pockets. He could be wearing a gun holster; I can't tell. I make a best guess that he isn't and go straight to business.

DONAL: 'The good news in a nutshell. I've got a cherry that's ripe and I need a cherry-picker and I hear you are the best in the business.'

[The language is a bit obtuse but Solomon picks up my meaning.]

SOLOMON: 'My work starts from the point of view that I have to plant the cherry. I plant it.'

DONAL: 'You plant it?'

SOLOMON: 'You bring the seed, I plant it and watch it grow… harvest it.'

DONAL: 'Reap what ye shall sow. Reap what ye shall sow.'

This elliptical conversation conveys that Solomon knows my background. The story we have fed him is that I am ex-SAS and a bodyguard to a lottery winner. I want to fleece my boss of his lucky fortune and plan to use Solomon's skills to that end. Solomon and I will receive an equal share of the loot.

Solomon has a stutter that is exacerbated, perhaps, by smoking some weed with his bodyguard. I am not sure, but sometimes I find it hard to understand him. When I don't, I just nod my head in agreement. Too many questions may be impolite. He says the way the deal will be worked out will mean that at the end of the scam it will look as if I have been ripped off as well, so that the finger of suspicion won't be pointed at me. I know that means he's probably planning to rip me off as well. He goes on to explain how to handle my 'boss'.

SOLOMON: 'The work starts from the time you leave this meeting and you get back to Manchester. He is going to ask you how your meeting went… You have to

introduce the business to him and let his greed
bring him in. I need him to take the bait.'

Solomon is my guide and I pay attention to his every word.

DONAL: 'So it's just like fishing? I haven't seen this in action
            but I've heard about it. I mean, do they really take
            the bait...?'
SOLOMON: 'Yes.'
DONAL: 'I'll believe it when I see it...'
SOLOMON: 'The storyline could be that the people you met in
            London are people you know through... being a
            bodyguard, and one of them used to be a personal
            bodyguard to Mobutu from Zaire, you know? So
            he is the one who has told you about this business
            and you met with him and Mobutu's son in
            London...'

The fraudsters use all the information in the public domain to give
credibility to their ruse. For this one they plan to say that ex-Zairian
President Mobutu took a lot of money with him to Ghana, where he
stayed briefly after he was deposed. Mobutu was notorious for milk-
ing his country of millions and it has been well reported that he took
huge sums of foreign reserves out of the country when he left. He
eventually left Ghana for Kenya, where he died. Solomon suggests
that there is a huge amount of money still in Ghana and we can use
this possibility to interest our lottery winner in helping Solomon to
extract the money for a healthy commission. Solomon and his
friends will pretend to be the dead president's son and part of the
dead president's entourage to give the scam a veneer of authority.

I am to pretend to my boss that I am planning to help get the
money out myself, but I'm having problems because my bank
accounts can't handle that kind of money without arousing
suspicion. Slowly I am to entice him to offer his support to the

'investment' opportunity and then Solomon will arrange another meeting to move the fraud on. Ideally he would like my boss to meet the 'dead president's son' (an actor – maybe Solomon himself), who would discuss the business arrangements with my lottery winner on the road to fleecing him.

I can hardly believe what I'm hearing. It's all true. These scams do happen and this man sitting in front of me pulls them off. He carries all the trappings of wealth – expensive watch, plush suit and fine shoes – and has obviously done this before. It seems greed is a powerful force; powerful enough to bring smart men down. I hope greed will also bring Solomon down.

I twirl my phone nervously around and then stop – it can't be helping the sound quality. It doesn't seem appropriate to move upstairs to the business suite, so we stay put on the sofa by the window. The cameras are rolling, I hope. As well as the people inside, we are being filmed from a Volvo in the car park – our seating arrangements having been worked out carefully beforehand. Solomon continues to expand on his plan for the scam for our benefit.

'Just tell him that the [son's] bodyguard has come to you. They escaped to Ghana with millions when he was toppled and the money is still lying in Ghana and they need somebody with the right accounts to move the money. There is a little bit of expense involved but very small.'

He explains that when the mark gets to Ghana, the 'pretend' Mobutu entourage will pull the black money scam on him and when he returns to London they will begin the cash extortion racket. At this moment, an apparently spurned lover walks into the lobby carrying flowers and deposits them in the corner of the lobby near us. The only unusual thing is that the flowers are in a vase – not a pretty vase but a beautiful camera – one of the very special vases from the unused conference room. He looks embarrassed, not so much because he (Colin, another producer) has been stood up by a girl, but because Alex has convinced him to ham up that role. I reflect that it is just as well our Nigerian friends are stoned because this side of bacon would get kicked out of Equity pronto. I bite my lip to keep a straight face and try to keep my mind on the business in hand.

SOLOMON: 'So let's be specific about the money. I think we should tell him something about seventy-five million.'
DONAL: 'Seventy-five million ?'
SOLOMON: 'Seventy-five million dollars and he gets 30 per cent.'

My boss stands to make nearly twenty-five million dollars if he joins Solomon in this ruse. I have a good idea that my lottery winner will go along with the scam. It is not just one scam but several merged into one. The scam mutates and evolves as necessary.

SOLOMON: 'He's going to bite the bait?'
DONAL: 'The thing is: one, he is not short of money; two, I am a Svengali figure, so he's in my palm... I'll pull him in.'

The meeting ends when I say that I have to go on to another engagement. Arrangements will be made in a while for another get-together. It seems that Solomon is happy with me. I hope he is persuaded by my acting. I have to say, a lot of the time, I'm not. There is more than one side of bacon walking around this hotel.

16th September 1998

There are beginners and there are absolute beginners. And then there is me. Technical things baffle me. Even the elementary technicalities of covert filming were learned over countless hours of fiddling and fumbling and getting it wrong over the last five years of occasional undercover work. Photography with its jargon of 'stops', 'buttons' and 'aperture' is beyond me. Way beyond. I need a lesson before I can palm myself off on the fashion world as a photographer. My tutor is Andy, a top London photographer.

'Andy, I don't need to be able to take a photograph, just look like a photographer.' I don't tell him why I need to play the role, I just tell him that I have to and he is happy with that.

Obliging and breathless with embarrassment at my paltry efforts, Andy nonetheless brings me through the actors' Equity guide to looking like a photographer. There are lots of technical phrases being bandied about. I nod and acquiesce to the terminology – like I understand. Andy looks at me hopefully. 'So, the big number equals the small hole and that's the way the aperture works, you see?' Not a muscle moves on my face. Eventually a quizzical look from Andy elicits a deadpan response. 'I haven't a clue, mate,' I say. There is a lot of work to be done.

17th September 1998

Solomon has been in contact. He is anxious to see a return on his advice. A message is relayed to him. 'The cherry tree is still ripe and there is still a need for a top-class cherry-picker.' Solomon is pleased. There is another meeting in the offing. It is all going to plan, for the moment.

I talk to my mom this evening. By increments her eyesight is improving, although there have been so many rollercoaster rides of hope and despair on the way to the loss of sight in her other eye that we – my family – have given some thoughts to preparing for the worst. She, however, refuses to give in to such a grey perspective and fights continually against unseasonably realistic medical assessments. For now she's winning the battle of hope over expectation.

23rd September 1998

Jason returns from his holiday and I head off to London Fashion Week. I am almost sad to leave. We've made progress and now I can't capitalize on it until I come back from the whirligig of fashion. However, Paul, as ever, will continue to plan and tickle the belly of the beast until my return. He will maintain a presence around Jason's hinterland while I am away.

A couple of days ago I went out and bought some designer clothes, a small wardrobe that would help me fit into my role. Well, I didn't – my producer Colin did, dragging me around the West End shops forcing me into trendy, *GQ*-type gear: sleek black creations, tee-shirts and v-neck tops and the obligatory combat trousers. Fashion trends did me a great favour when combat came back into fashion – there is nothing better for hiding tapes and recording batteries than the stylish military streetwear. We had to ensure that not only were the clothes fashionable and ones a top-notch photographer would wear, but also that they could be adapted to hide secret cameras. For every top we decided on, Colin would buy three: one for a colour camera, one for a black-and-white and one dummy. I might have to change these clothes several times a day depending on the light and the threat of being caught (sometimes I don't wear a camera if I think the risk of exposure is too high).

Really, I haven't got a clue about what to wear, whichever the field. Last time I went shopping for some hooligan gear by myself, I was laughed out of the office. Paul now does all my hooligan shopping. Poor fashion sense doesn't help at all when you're trying to infiltrate fashion, but it's a handicap I hope to overcome.

I am armed with a rented camera – a bona fide Nikon F4, not a secret one (although I will be carrying those, too) – which I struggle to fit together and load with film. My one half-day photography lesson has not done much good. It looks like I am trying to knit a jumper rather than take a picture. More important than that, though, is my preparation for a meeting with some of the main subjects of my investigation, two of the Moonsinners, a group of playboys who work for the nightclubs of Milan. It might sound like an obscure angle to take on a story, but Lisa and Colin assure me that these guys are the way into the whole fashion business.

It is time for me to forget all about my drug-dealer, football-hooligan persona for a while and slip into a world that, on the face of it, couldn't be more different. The transition between the two lives will be difficult but for the next three to four weeks it will be my only focus. There are a couple of things I must do immediately to make the transition such as pull back on my bad language. Mixing with the likes of Jason is rubbing off. I must watch my every word. It will make a pleasant change not to hear language like that too often. More than that, though, I must change my personality. Gone are the taciturn, brooding and violent characteristics of my football persona, and newly created is a bumptious, bubbly and off-the-scale, larger-than-life character who will entice and intrigue the eclectic range of people that I am going to meet in this new environment. An off-the-peg personality for a *prêt à porter* world.

24th September 1998

The fashion world descends upon The Metropolitan hotel in London. This is the social centre, by proxy, of London Fashion Week, and in order to put myself at the heart of this world in one hit I take a room at the hotel. It is expensive, but in the long run I hope it will prove to be a short cut and provide me with the necessary credentials.

Lisa and Colin, who have been out in Milan hyping my name to the PRs, have encouraged them to come to London for Fashion Week and meet their photographer friend Mac, who is not only brilliant and talented but very generous with his hospitality. Apart from the lies about my prowess, this meeting should give me credibility and allow me to cement the relationship further in Milan Fashion Week, which follows on from London.

The first to arrive is Diego. Lisa brings him to meet me in the bar of the hotel. She is well known in Milan and the PRs are comfortable with her. They think that Lisa has been a model – and we have set her up with her own portfolio of photographs to give the story authenticity. She has written for all the main UK broadsheets and did an article for *The Sunday Times* on how to transform your look into that of a model's. Indeed, we used the same techniques to create Lisa's bogus catwalk portfolio.

She had described Diego to me as looking like Rumpelstiltskin, with long straggly hair, a bent posture, an awkward gait and built-up boots. He also, she informed me, wore a trademark bandanna. We are introduced and I see what she means. Pony-tailed, wearing shades and a long fawn jacket down to his ankles, he is instantly recognizable. He has penetrating brown eyes, makes an impression when he enters the room and has a certain charm about him. Diego is a permanent fixture on the Milan fashion scene, where he is known by the nickname 'Capitano Belvio' ('Captain Beast'), apparently because he is not very discerning about who he sleeps with.

In case he comes to my hotel room after our meeting, there are cameras hidden in suitcases around my suite and I am wearing a tee-shirt cam. This first meeting is of huge significance. I must not get it wrong. One slip early on and the door to the fashion world will be very firmly shut, putting an end to the story. It would be a real shame because Lisa and Colin have already done a good deal of research and everything is in place for me.

The PRs have been told that I am a top 'reportage' photographer, who is interested in fashion for a possible photographic exhibition. I have no confidence in my ability to make moves in this kind of company, but am trying to puff myself up. In these circles, appearance is everything – though what chance I have as a small, overweight Irishman with absolutely no fashion sense I dare not try to calculate. I decide to give reality a rain-check and give it my best shot.

Diego and I greet each other and I get the drinks in. He is delighted to be in London and to avail himself of my hospitality. He has no idea of my motivation. If I didn't know what he is really about, I might even have liked him on a superficial basis.

He is best described as Bohemian. He describes himself in more poetic terms as 'the shadow that moves beneath'. Diego, not wanting to play himself down in terms of morality, claims to be a 'turned' angel. His weakness for women has depraved him and he is quite open about it. He jokes that he has two angel wings, one black and one white. Unfortunately, the black one always upstages the white one and the weakness of the flesh always wins. I find the whole scenario surreal.

25th September 1998

I share some sandwiches with Diego in my hotel room – the cameras are switched on by remote-control – and continue to probe him about what exactly he does for a job. He explains that PRs usually work in packs of five or six, taking models to Milan's exclusive clubs and sitting them at tables with wealthy clients. It is not exactly prostitution, but Diego confides that he can arrange to get girls and put them in a position to sleep with clients. For this he is sometimes rewarded by clients with gifts such as cocaine. He is open about his drug use, which, it seems, is part and parcel of fashionable Milanese life.

If he doesn't qualify as a proper pimp, he certainly makes money out of exploiting the models. Both the club he works for and its rich patrons pay handsomely for Diego's services.

'The more women you have, the more money you collect,' he explains. Not that Diego is really in it for the money. Sex is what it's all about for him. He is, after all, a Moonsinner, one of the exclusive band of PRs who work the Milan clubs, reaping the sexual benefits. He's happy to elaborate:

'What you have to understand [is] that... every girl wants you to fuck her, every single woman in the world wants you to fuck her. They just need a good reason. You just give them the right reason, or make them think that you are giving them a good reason and they will fuck you, no matter if they are married, no matter if they are babies, no matter if they are working, no matter if they are younger or older than you. Just give them the right reason.'

I didn't ask for the PR guide to seduction but that is what I get.

Diego is only just warming up, however. What follows makes foot-ball hooligans sound like polite company.

The PRs have a contest and a league table to see how many models they can sleep with during the year.

'It's like, the more you fuck, if you are able to use your fucking in the right way, the more popularity you get, the higher your rank, the more the club pays for you.'

Diego's English isn't perfect, but there's no mistaking what he's saying. He tells me that the Moonsinners created the contest in order to 'stimulate' themselves because at the end of a fashion season they get bored of sex and need to spice up their interactions with the models.

It's a points contest, with its own unique scoring system. Only card-carrying models from well-known agencies count, and they must be in work. Diego is very insistent on the standard of his model companions.

'Every time you go with a model, you give yourself a score, depending on what you've been doing. If it's like a French kiss, it's one point. If she gives you a blow job or you eat her pussy, it's four points. If you fuck her normally, it's six points. If you fuck her up the ass, it's nine points. If you fuck her with your friend, it's ten points. If you fuck her and her friend – if she's a model – you get twenty points. So for three girls, it's like thirty points and stuff.'

Diego's good friend and fellow Moonsinner, Oliver, is coming to London tonight. He has contacts in the upper echelons of the fashion world and he is now also doing some work for a major fashion house in Milan. Oliver is a PR of ten years' standing and Diego has much respect for him. 'He's really from the Old Guard, and he's considered one of the most beautiful guys in town… Go out with him, it's cool.'

Cool? Has the word lost all meaning? More and more I feel as if I am on another planet. I just want to go as far away from Diego and his friends as possible. It is not to be, however. I've got to put on a designer shirt and mingle.

I spend the evening rubbing shoulders among the fashion élite in trendy bars and restaurants. It doesn't sound like hard work, but it is. I feel incredibly uncomfortable in this environment. It reminds me of being a learner hooligan at the World Cup – completely lost and floundering hopelessly. I grit my teeth and paste on a smile. I am Mac, an international, highly respected photographer, I tell myself. Introduced by Lisa, I shake hands, double-kiss cheeks and drink champagne. It's important that people get to know my face. So many of them will troop on to Milan and Paris. You never know just what dividends a sighting here or a sense of familiarity there can bring.

I meet the infamous Oliver at a late-night fashion event. He has a firm handshake and is warm and polite. I avail him of some of my hospitality and we end up back at The Metropolitan hotel chatting into the early hours. I don't know what to make of him yet. Saw Liam Gallagher tonight, too, in the Met bar. I didn't know what to make of him either.

26th September 1998

My first appearance as a pretend photographer is the John Rocha show at the Natural History Museum in Kensington. Unfortunately, I don't just have to pretend to be a photographer socially, I also have to attend the shows and be seen to do my job.

There is an etiquette in the rat pack, but it escapes me. Apparently every main photographer has a little marked-out perimeter fence in chalk on the floor, facing full frontal onto the cat-walk, and it is heresy to stray beyond your boundaries. Of course, that is what I do, by accident. I strike up a conversation with a Scottish photographer and pretend that someone has wiped out my chalk marks.

'It's getting nasty in the pack,' he says, adding sorrowfully, 'I can't believe it's come to this.'

I shake my head in mutual disbelief. I am busking it. I fumble with my camera and film. It is truly idiotic. No one notices – they're all too busy – apart from Colin, my producer, who looks on incredulously. Colin has got permission to view the shows as a film cameraman who is doing a documentary on fashion.

When I can't gain access through my ficticious magazine *Polkadot*, I also gain accreditation as a photographer hired by a film crew for a documentary about fashion. I thought that it may pose problems, but no one is interested in looking at your accreditation. It's all about being seen and not much else. Never before has someone so incompetent been in the company of so many fine photographers. Sadly, there is no osmosis effect. I am hopeless from start to finish and it is a triumph just to turn the camera on. I am clearly creating a very weak alibi. I have had one short lesson as a photographer, but some of these cameras are complicated. My Nikon F4 is rented. I tape over the rental name and pretend it is mine. No one is looking. No one cares. I'm glad I paid more attention to learning the essentials of Chelsea history than I did to the technicalities of the camera. After Rocha, I meet up with my boys again.

It is late Saturday evening and I am with Diego and Oliver in my hotel room. They are relaxed and regale me with more tales from the black heart of Milan. One is particularly horrific. Oliver sets the scene. He reiterates Diego's detailed explanation of the points contest, laying great emphasis on the 'nine pointer', anal sex.

Diego then takes up the story. 'To give yourself the score you have to pump at least ten times,' he elaborates. 'If you pump like six times, then you don't get the points. So with this girl, she didn't want that after the first two times. She was like [in a young girl's voice], "No, no, please stop, it hurts".'

As an aside, he says that he was counting, and laughs. In a higher pitch he continues, 'No, no, let me up. Stop, please.' But Diego had not achieved his ten penetrations and no cries from the model were going to stop him until he had. After the requisite ten he pretended contrition and said, 'Let's stop, I don't want to hurt you.'

By way of explanation, he qualifies what he feels is a hilarious story by telling me, 'I couldn't give a fuck'.

27th September 1998

It's Sunday and sleep is an absent friend. We have strategy meetings and continue to make our mark in this world. This evening I go to Alexander McQueen's show. I go as a photographer. I have no interest in clothes, I never have, but his show is special. His show is theatre and it is showmanship way beyond anything I have ever seen. Models walk into the amphitheatre and are sprayed with paint by robotic spray guns. Oliver and Diego attend, too, and they feel increasingly comfortable in my company. There is no suspicion about me or my credentials whatsoever. Thankfully they can't see me struggling to shovel the film into the camera. In the show I see a leading British model, Carolyn Park. If you make the McQueen show, you are certainly in the big time. I wonder if I will meet any of these models later on my fashion trail.

28th September 1998

For Fashion Week I am using the same Mercedes that I have rented for my role as a football hooligan (having first removed the St George air freshener and the Protestant music tapes). This is to underline the fact – or in my case, the fantasy – that I am a leading photographer. Diego and I are driven in the Mercedes to lunch by one of my colleagues, who is acting as a chauffeur to maximize the impact. Oliver left for Milan this morning and Diego is due to fly out tomorrow.

We go to a small Italian eatery in Queensway, London. We are getting to know each other just that little bit more every time we sit down and talk. I try and probe him on his relationships with models and his fellow Italian playboys. He in turn tries to probe me about photography. Diego often pretends to be a photographer and believes that it is a great way of getting close to models. He is fascinated by my job and asks if I use it as a means to bed women. I demur for effect.

Diego – who calls himself 'a pussy-hunter with style' – feels in control when he talks about women. 'For me it's a cult. A religion, like what [when] you do believe in God. I believe in women... I love them more than myself, that's why I need to take their measure. I can infiltrate them as well.'

He elaborates on his job as a PR. 'You never stop being a PR. I mean, twenty-four hours and seven [days a week] you're working... Since you wake up, your only purpose is like meeting people and trying to find out if they can be good for the club or not.'

Interspersed in the conversation, I get (previously arranged) calls on the mobile, and ham it up as if I am making photographic appointments and organizing shoots. I have to be careful because you wouldn't have to know much about photography to know more than me. I have a few stock phrases and most certainly over-use them, but Diego does not seem to notice that. He continues to talk about the PRs, regaling me with a story about some of them having sex with a young model who was so drunk she had collapsed and didn't even know her own name. Diego says that he has come across people in Milan who have spiked the drinks of young models in order to sleep with them – a fact that is confirmed by models Lisa has spoken to in the course of our research. This is the type of behaviour that originally got me interested in what was going on in Milan. All the same, it is distressing to hear first hand.

The PRs are not interested in women unless they have a model-ling contract. It's like a driving licence. That modelling licence makes the model a lucrative asset to the PR, a person worth know-ing and somebody a PR would get paid to take to a Milan night-club. The problem is that many of the models in Milan are very young. The young models are supposed to be looked after and pro-tected from the traditional vices of the fashion world – vices that are part of the life and times of the Milan PRs.

With the PRs in town, we're working almost round the clock. Whenever they're awake, we need to know where they are. Whenever they're asleep, we need to prepare for the next filming opportunity. What with babysitting Diego and Oliver, the party scene at night and the shows during the day, plus all our technical work, I'm left with about three hours' sleep a night. I am in such a state of exhaustion and high tension that I am not forgetting to do things, but forgetting that I have ever done them. I need to pace myself, I realize. Milan is just around the corner.

I squeeze in time to call my mom at home. For the moment her sight is safe. The eye pressure is stable and her one and only working eye is now furrowing through magazines and books as usual. Against all expectations she's pulled through. Thank God.

30th September 1998

I leave London looking and feeling like a refugee and arrive looking just as bad. I am haggard and my Celtic complexion has given way to a sickly, ash-coloured pallor. For the last week I've been living on a diet of cigarettes, sandwiches and coffee, and it shows. Not only that, but the effort of maintaining 'Mac', my larger-than-life photographer character, is beginning to take its toll. My bounciness and enthusiasm are looking a little jaded now and sometimes I feel as if I'm running out of stories to tell. The danger is that the PR guys may end up getting bored and lose interest in me.

Despite my tiredness I am out tonight being entertained by Diego. He introduces me to Milan and many of the other PRs. We meet them at a restaurant where many of the models are brought by the PRs before they are expected to entertain the wealthy clients who pay for their attentions at the late nightclubs. I meet one PR who tells me about some of the young models. He was dating a girl for a couple of days when he found out she was thirteen. He says that he felt like a paedophile. Nonetheless he stayed with her.

Diego paves my path for me and I am made welcome. I arrive at one of the clubs and Diego has already made some arrangements. As he tells me, the girls have no choice. They will be brought to my table and seated. He says that 'the customer is king.' And they are young. One is fourteen. But this isn't her first night here. Earlier, as a thirteen-year-old, she was also in the club taking orders from the PRs. She didn't seem disturbed by it, but at her age she just didn't understand.

1st October 1998

While I am meeting the élite of the fashion world and attending more shows, I receive bad news on the football front. Jason is leaving his flat. 'Aaaaargh,' I think. I can feel the pain in Milan. This could bring problems. Luckily, though, it's not far. He has told Paul he is just moving down the way. How inconvenient of him, I think, how inconsiderate of him to be so uncooperative in his own downfall. Really, Jason, do you not know what efforts have gone into becoming your neighbour and then you have the effrontery to up sticks and leave. Jason is living in *The Truman Show* – a real-life version.

5th October 1998

While I am chasing around like a lunatic, Lisa, who has good contacts here, is sounding out young models and getting their side of the story. Already she has recorded some PRs trying to bully a drunken young model at a club and has frequently taxied models home to get them out of trouble. On one of her expeditions she ends up at a dinner for a group of Elite models. Elite is one of the world's biggest and most respected model agencies. Present at the dinner is Gérald Marie, one of the owners of the agency, who was formerly married to supermodel Linda Evangelista. At the meal, in front of his colleagues, he tries to engage Lisa in conversation about the size of their penises. Lisa is carrying a bag camera for her evidence-gathering, so the exchange is recorded.

LISA: 'The biggest what?'

GÉRALD: 'The biggest dick, yes?'

LISA: 'No, I just came for a drink.'

GÉRALD: 'He [pointing at a colleague] has dick, it is like the arm of a kid and the head of a cat. You want to start with him, or with him?'

Lisa responds inoffensively that she wants a glass of wine. Gérald says she can have it after, and laughs. This is our introduction to Gérald Marie.

That night he brings his corporate companions, some of whom work for him, to what he calls a 'whorebar'. Lisa phones me to keep me up to speed with developments. She wangles an invitation and a lift to a late-night drinking-and-showgirl establishment called Williams, and tells them she is going to meet her friend (me) there.

I arrive and use Lisa's presence to gain entry into Gérald Marie's private circle. We chat intermittently about sport. He says I look like a rugby player. I start to tell him that I am Irish-American when he lights on the word 'Irish', and that's when I drop the American label and run with what works for him. He loves the Irish and he loves rugby. There are not many people in the fashion industry who share his interest in rugby and a bond is created. By the time Lisa and I leave, he has given me his international mobile number and suggests I link up with him during Paris Fashion Week. I say I'll see him there, but I don't seriously believe he means it.

6th October 1998

Gerald Marie is the President of Elite Europe and over the years has been instrumental in the careers of Linda Evangelista, Naomi Campbell, Iman and thousands of other models worldwide. He contributed significantly to creating the supermodel phenomenon by marketing them for the first time as a unit. The supermodels, in his hands, became bigger names than the designers they were working for.

It was a radical transformation for the industry and the predominant theme in fashion in the 1990s. Elite, now the biggest name in the modelling world, is famous for its search for new talent. Every year over 350,000 young girls from fifty-seven countries compete in the Elite Model Look Competition from which Elite chooses many of its new models and fresh talent.

I had learned a little about the industry today. Getting to know Gérald Marie meant getting to know the business of fashion. But he represents the aristocracy of fashion and I can't imagine that I can get to know him well enough and long enough to unlock the secrets of fashion – though that may well be what it will take.

7th October 1998

A discussion is going on among the production team in the foyer of the hotel. They are talking about me. They think that I may be getting too tired to do my job. Since we touched down in Milan the pace has been relentless. I dismiss all suggestions of exhaustion and insist I'm fine. As I leave, there is a crash and a body 'reverb' like the ones in cartoons. I have walked smack into the glass partition separating reception from the outer lobby. My face marks the glass like the Turin Shroud. The imprint is left for days. The imprint of the glass on my face lasts for days, too. I guess in retrospect I was shattered. Rather me than the glass, though. Of all the risks I take, to get hurt walking into a glass door would be a tough one to live down.

This afternoon I have another meeting with Diego in a street café. The set-up is in place. There is a hired van across the street with a small camera trained on my table, in addition to my body-rig camera. I am drinking coffee when Diego strolls up.

'How you doing, Mac?' (All undercover journalists should use a one-syllable name tag because, if people can remember your name, they feel they have a little social stake in you and it makes it easier for them to interact with you.)

Diego is still very enthusiastic about pressing his photographic credentials and is keen to leave the PR world behind him. It's proving hard for him; as he explains, you get trapped into the role. He is smoking. So am I. I wave the smoke across my chest in case he sees the lens in the centre of my tee-shirt.

Diego is genuinely warm and almost philosophical but, deep down, he is still a PR. He can't resist telling me how he manages to bed so many beautiful women. 'The secret is one hundred per cent honesty, 'cos they love it... They love to be treated like shit.' He has slept with hundreds of models and some of them make the front covers of mainstream fashion magazines. His courtship technique is to shower them with attention, then be nasty, leaving them wanting more. 'You have to beat them and give them roses'. I am perplexed and I show it. Diego tries another simile. 'You have to give them... sugar, like to horses, to make them keep running.' Working his way through an entire stable of models is exhausting, even for Diego.

'Basically, it was girls before, girls, girls, girls, always girls and that is why I'm like over-digested that, sick of it... I'm still totally into pussy, I mean I'm not getting gay, I'm not getting tired of fucking or anything... but I don't have the energy of when I was eighteen...' He is fatigued by young models now. 'The new girls are fifteen. You know, I want big girls now. I don't want to fuck like young innocents that know nothing about nothing...they're not fine anymore. They would be fine if I didn't have them before but I [already] did that stage.'

A good PR can earn two million lira (roughly £740) a month and some get a percentage of the club's takings. It's not a high salary, but gives a PR an expensive lifestyle, with models and drink as part of the job. He says he lives in his car, an old white Volvo estate, but spends most of his time in the company of the models he is beginning to detest. 'It's super-depressing. It made me get to the point in which I almost start hating girls.'

Diego's eyes never speak. They are behind dark glasses. I can't tell his facts from his fiction. I suppose he can't tell mine apart either. It's just as well. We have a conversation about photography.

He seems to know as little as me. We start throwing technical photographic terms at each other like a cowboy shoot-out, though with my volubility levels I am considerably quicker on the draw. It's something that Colin has had to warn me about. Apparently, my fashion alter-ego is becoming so inflated that it's stopping me doing my job properly. Later, I get a dressing down.

'The trouble is, having befriended the right people, you now have to give them a chance to talk. Your character, though, is so bombastic and cartoonish that most people can barely get a word in.' He tells me to 'rev my performance down a little'.

8th October 1998

Billboards the size of buildings announce throughout Milan that it is Gianfranco Ferré's twentieth anniversary. His show has attracted many of the *Hello!* celebrities and your very favourite and most incompetent photographer is there in his full unwashed glory. Donald Trump doesn't think much of my attempt to photograph him, though, especially when I have to stop mid-shoot because my flash isn't working. A second visit and a second request elicits this reply from '*The* Donald': 'Just take the fucking photograph.'

My post-show photographic attempts are better. I catch supermodel Naomi Campbell getting ready to leave after the show and ask if I can take her picture. She asks me not to show her smoking. 'Sure thing,' I say, clicking away. I enjoy my brief interaction with her. I am here because it's important to be seen doing my job. After all, this bit isn't too arduous, even if I am a mere pretender.

10th October 1998

The camera is a strange confessional. When people have a lens trained on them, they feel compelled to talk. This is a technique I am not aware of until it happens with Lorenzo.

Lorenzo is a twenty-eight-year-old PR of ten years' standing and a Moonsinner. I interview him under the guise of relaxing him for a photograph in the back of Shocking Nightclub. There is film in my camera, a camera strapped to my chest, a tape recorder taped around my body and a mini-disc in my pocket. Colin, who has a bag camera, is also witnessing the scene. Colin is supposed to be my friend and a music video talent-spotter.

'What do PRs do?' I begin.

'Yeah, chasing after models twenty-four hours a day.' He tosses his mane of dramatically flowing hair.

'What a job, fantastic,' I enthuse. I continue to try to build up evidence of the system in Milan. Lorenzo says that he meets the models at castings, agencies – everywhere, in fact. This is important because it shows that some of the agencies know how the PRs work and, in some cases, facilitated it.

'Let's have a look.' He points to the preliminary Polaroids.

I am caught out. 'Yeah, absolutely.'

Lorenzo is downcast. 'But I look bad.'

'No, no, you're very photogenic.'

He is not having it. 'This is ugly.'

I flannel madly. 'Oh no, no, no – but in black and white, you know, the contours of your face and shadows and the contrast will really come out. Yeah. That's great. Those colours will look really good when they're processed.'

'Really?' He wants to believe me.

'Yeah, bit of cross-processing, you know, a few ND9 filters you know, fine,' I explain, struggling with some techno-photographic speak. The charade never stops.

I have lured Lorenzo and some of the other guys into a blue-painted corridor running to a fire exit, purportedly to take some atmospheric photographs, but actually because it's the only place quiet enough for my mike to pick up what they're saying. 'This is the Moonsinners' lounge, it's an historical room,' Lorenzo says. It is a blue escape route where they have done drugs and had sex for years. It is narrow and unappealing. He is, in his own words, 'The chief', and has been winning the PRs' points league table for the last few years. On his finger he wears the Moonsinner's ring with its distinctive insignia, a half-moon and a star in solid silver. The ring is specially imported from Mexico and defines you as a member of one of the most influential and seedy gangs in Italy. It's not a secret club, far from it. At three o'clock every morning, a PR will broadcast an announcement: 'Moonsinners are in the House'. The announcement sparks a rousing cheer. The Moonsinners are famous in Milan, but not many know about their points table.

I dig deeper and ask Lorenzo about which model bookers he works with. Suddenly there is a switch, and he looks uncomfortable. I have asked too many questions too fast. His intuition rails against it and he clams up. I start to soft-pedal him and bring him back into the fold, aware of the damage I might have caused.

Lino is another PR but he plays higher stakes. He runs the club and acts as a PR as well. He isn't there when I interrogate Lorenzo, but I meet him afterwards. Keen to join in, Lino exclaims that there are only two things in life: 'Drugs and pussy'. And a brief job description for the camera? 'I give drinks to girls and fuck them.'

13th October 1998

I am still very tired from the unrelenting schedule. I am now sick. My travelling companions are Lemsip and flu germs. Back at home, I have just enough time to water some flowers and watch a couple of episodes of *The Simpsons* on TV before the airport calls.

Later that night, I fly from London to Paris, to join the fashion show jamboree and hopefully to meet Gérald Marie.

14th October 1998

The fashion feeding frenzy begins again. Colin wants me to capitalize on my new-found friendship with Gérald Marie, but I am too shy to ring up total strangers and ask them for a drink. It may be normal behaviour in fashion, but it's not me. Colin pushes me. I keep putting it off. Eventually, cringing, I psyche myself up and call.

Unbelievably, Gérald invites me to lunch at his favourite restaurant on Rue de Cherche Midi in downtown Paris, a short distance from Elite's headquarters. Oh, my God, I think. This is where the upper echolons of the fashion world meet up. Why am I here? I pull myself together and organize my secret camera and mini-disc recorder. A taxi takes me there and drops me outside.

I am early. I hang about and then do the professional thing and say to the waiter that I am there to meet Gérald Marie. They know him; he is a favourite son. I am seated at a prime table close to the door to wait for him.

He arrives and greets me with a warm handshake. Three other men join us and Gérald introduces me as a friend who he met in a whorehouse. He regales us with stories of his night with the prostitutes, joking that he ran out of condoms and had to send the porter to get some more for him. His party took four prostitutes back to his hotel and they swapped the women among themselves (work collegues). 'We took four in a big room together, Ching (denoting sex, I figure) 'You finished with yours, send her to me. We run out of condoms and we call down to reception. You know, they get us condoms in three minutes, a box. Yes, Gérald Marie, call me lion!' He is proud of his sexual exploits and tells his friends that 'You have to go there. It's not very romantic,' he adds, but says the girls are 'beautiful'. Staggered, I disentangle myself and return to meet Colin.

20th October 1998

I am flying home. My head is in a whirl. In the course of our fashion investigation, the team and I have filmed nearly 115 hours' worth of material. We have spent thousands of hours trawling nightclubs, fashion shows and restaurants being seen and making connections, hoping for an evidential crumb here and there. We've got some and we need to go away and digest it. Meanwhile, it's time to get off this merry-go-round and forget about fashion. I have to mentally readjust to think football. No more hugs and kisses and 'ciaos'. It's time for some ruthless bad-boy language and low-key body movement.

27th October 1998

Jason has been hard to find since he left our neighbourhood. He is erratic and that is not good for us. Having tracked down his work-place and tyre business, we decide that we might have to interest him in a little proposition. Today we go to Jason's tyre yard and say we need his advice. Paul takes the lead.

'Listen, mate, I was thinkin' of investing in a van courier business. I'm sorting out the figures. Couldn't give me a price on twenty sets of van tyres?'

Jason's face pales slightly and he inhales deeply. 'It's gonna be a whack, mate.'

'Just work out the figures and we'll have a chat later in the week.'

'Yeah, yeah, mate. Cushty, mate.'

The plan is to give Jason as many reasons as possible to keep him interested in Paul and me. Chelsea is going abroad next week and it would be very useful to be able to travel with Jason. His stamp of approval would guarantee us access into the heart of the Chelsea Old Guard, and the time away with Jason would mean that we could debrief him thoroughly over a couple of days. We know that Jason is going, but has not yet made his travel arrangements. This is something we will try to exploit over the next couple of days.

28th October 1998

There is no idea better than a borrowed one. The film *ID* draws loosely upon the failed undercover operation that the police ran on the Chelsea Head-hunters in the eighties. In this fictionalized account, one of the officers pretends that he can't read or write to disarm the hooligans he is infiltrating.

If it could work once – if only on the silver screen – then it could work twice, we decide, this time in the field. The plan is for Paul to pretend to be illiterate so that he can ask Jason to travel over with him to Copenhagen to help him get through the airports. I will already be in Copenhagen with the secret camera gear ready to roll when they turn up in Denmark. It wouldn't be good enough to meet up with Jason over there because it would be very hard to find him, particularly regarding his propensity for making trouble.

There may be a chink in our master plan, however, if Jason has seen the film (and the odds are that he has). Will he smell a rat when he talks to his 'illiterate' pal? It's a chance we don't have to take, but we decide to risk it.

29th October 1998

In the pubs around Hampton Hill Paul sows the seed: he can't read. This is sent in directions that he knows will go right back to Jason. Hopefully he will hear about Paul's unfortunate problem before Paul confesses it himself. I suggest that Paul buys some Ladybird books as props for the back of the car.

31st October 1998

It's raining. The Chelsea Old Guard are not happy. The match against Aston Villa has been cancelled and their afternoon entertainment is off. We are at their regular haunt, a pub called the Fulham Dray, off Fulham Broadway. Jason is there, but he is not very communicative, at least not with me. I am not sure if this is because he is suspicious of me or if he is just brooding because the game is off. He turns away and speaks to a mate. The talk is about violence. It is the first time that I hear him speak of organized violence.

ANON: 'We could go down to Victoria.'

JASON: 'They won't stay about, they'll only be forty-handed. I wanna fucking have a walkabout to see if they're about then, the cunts.'

Jason is not a happy bunny. Around Stamford Bridge he acts a bit odd. Normal interaction with him, certainly before a game, is not possible. His pre-match routine is an all-consuming one and it has been upset. Someone is going to pay for it. The Villa are in town and seem the most likely targets.

DONAL: 'I bet Villa have scarpered.'

JASON: 'No, they're about. Fulham Old Bill have already pulled one of our lads. They're [Villa] going over to Victoria but all my lot are over at Victoria. They'll [Villa] get smashed to pieces.'

Jason is sideways to me as he is speaking. He is distracted, I keep saying to myself, or else he is partially blanking me. For the moment, to keep my confidence high, I assume he's distracted. He continues talking to me, but not at me. I am wearing a secret camera and so is my BBC colleague Mike, who is here today with Paul and me. There must be hundreds in the pub and we are all squeezed together. My elbows protect my covert recorder and the cigarette continues to keep people from coming too close to my body. Occasionally a colleague, either Paul or Mike, will protect my camera rig by walking beside me to protect the side that is carrying the secret kit.

Jason is just still not sure of me, and the tapes, when we view them later, show him looking at me very strangely. He is not convinced. It doesn't all add up in his head – the way I have turned up at his pub, his club and his house. Fortunately, he doesn't act on his vague suspicions, perhaps because he is too focused on getting Villa. Naming some of the Chelsea Head-hunters who I have only seen on press hooligan photofits, he says they are on their way to Victoria.

At this stage I am not supposed to be interested in violence, only in football, so I don't ask too many questions. And when he goes for a wander I don't follow because the time is not quite right yet.

Football and violence are the primary focus of Jason's life. Everything else just serves those interests. In his head he is more loyal to 'Chels' than any of the paid mercenaries (players) that make up the team. Jason is with them for life, not just a couple of seasons. Today, it is apparent. In the pub he breathes in the air thick with smoke and bacon crisps and bitter breath and says, 'Can you feel it? It's blue through and through!'

Time is running out to introduce Jason to the great illiteracy idea, but he is too distracted today. Plus, it's not something he might be receptive to if he is in a suspicious mood. Better to wait, even if we are under pressure – we can't risk a complete blowout. It's going to have to be Monday.

2nd November 1998

Paul is off to see Jason. We are both psyched up for it, but this is not my moment. I am sharing Paul's anxiety, though. There is a lot depending on our ruse about Paul's illiteracy. He has been practising writing with his left hand: 'Ar u goin to Copenhargen – Paul'. It is almost illegible. It looks convincing. I pat him on the back and tell him to watch his grammar, then retire to my favourite café to wait with a quadruple espresso.

When Paul returns (after one false start; Jason isn't in the first time but he's back an hour later), his face has lost its tension. The hints we left dotted around Hampton have hit home. When Jason saw Paul he pre-empted his request with a wink and said straight off, 'You're not very good at travelling, mate, are ya?' Paul confessed to his problem with airports and got an immediate, 'No worries, mate, you can travel with me'. And that is a result. Jason and Chelsea are going abroad and we're going with them.

(The funny thing is that Jason himself has used the 'I can't read' scam, we find out later, to get himself off the hook with the DSS after a seven-year spell of unemployment. He, too, wrote with his left hand to convince them he was illiterate and couldn't get a job and he was sent to adult literacy classes for his pains. He kept his dole cheque.)

3rd November 1998

Paul and I visit Jason's garage for a final assurance that he is going. He is. After a brief chat about ticket prices, it's agreed that Paul and Jason will sort out their travel arrangements later. Despite these assurances, I won't really believe it until Jason is there with me in Copenhagen.

5th November 1998

Jason thinks I am in Amsterdam on 'business' and am flying in for the game and will meet up with Paul and him at the airport. In fact, Pip, Colin and I are already in Copenhagen, awaiting the arrival of Paul and Jason. I wake up with a knot in my belly. It is either a stomach ulcer or plain nerves. I suspect the latter. Hardly surprising – I am about to go on tour with the Chelsea Head-hunters. We have come a long way. There is still a long way to go, though.

We have heard from Paul, who has kept in touch discreetly with his mobile. I am worried about him. He is nervous but cautious. I'm sure he'll be all right as long as he remembers he's supposed to be illiterate. He has been turning his head away from all newspapers and ignoring departure signs. Jason is helping him and enjoying the role. This is good news. We can now track his movements and I will know definitely when he is arriving in Copenhagen.

En route Paul has sown a seed that will, hopefully, prove very useful later. He has told Jason that my brother was killed by the IRA. Clues such as this work fifty per cent of the time but, like advertising, you never know which fifty per cent.

I meet up with them at the airport right on schedule. Jason is in a hurry to get away. His head turns left and right checking for 'Chelsea Old Bill', as he puts it. We bail into a taxi and head for the city centre and an English bar, which seems to be a pre-arranged meeting point for the Chelsea Head-hunters.

Before the game we drink copious amounts of lager (an occupational hazard – I am still leaving half-empty bottles in an attempt to stay clear-headed). Jason leads us all in 'The Sash', a Loyalist song, and I hum along and join in the chorus where I can. The older Chelsea chants leave me bemused and where I struggle I concentrate on looking tough by smoking and drinking. The Old Guard joke about the last time they were in Denmark, when they smashed the place up. The English fans had attacked the Danish fans and, when they had finished with them, began fighting among themselves.

Jason regales them with old war stories. 'We were absolutely gassed and smashed to fuck. They [the police] come in and we're standing in the cells and everyone starts singing "Eng-er-land" and all these fucking mad songs in the cells.'

'You had a good weekend!' one says.

'Yeah, absolutely superb,' Jason agrees.

They discuss the Own Goal trial and revel in the massive compensation that some alleged Head-hunters received when they were released by the appeal court for wrongful conviction. There were some discrepancies in the police evidence that made their convictions unsafe.

Jason breaks off the conversation to shout, 'We've come home to have a war', loud and in received pronunciation for dramatic effect.

Jason chats about a football tour to Poland, where they visited Auschwitz and gave homage to their racism. Jason talks about his mate, Andy Frain, who went there with him.

'So they are having this tour thing.' Jason paints the scene animatedly. 'And they're talking to all these Jerries about what happened... blah blah.' He dismisses the history lesson from the tour guide as he describes taking a holiday snap of his friend doing a

Nazi salute. 'All the Jerries started going [mad].' His mate's response was, 'Fuck off, it's what I believe in.' Jason tells how, 'some Polish geezer started crying.' He wipes his eyes mockingly. The Polish man was upset when he saw the coats worn by some of the children who were killed at the camp. Andy Frain told the crying Polish visitor to 'Fuck off'. Jason continues with this story to his laughing audience. 'Next he's [Andy Frain] up on the roof acting like he's having a David Gower [shower] ...where they put the gas in.' Jason acts it out like an Ealing comedy. This was not the most offensive act Andy Frain committed. Apparently, he unzipped his jeans over an anonymous grave and wrote the word 'Nazi' in urine.

'I think I put the final nail in the coffin when... I was in the gas chamber and I was trying to get into the oven.' He tells his audience that he believes what he believes and that is that. 'And they're [the Jews] all come to Auschwitz to work their bollocks off and they're winding up with fuck all,' he laughs. 'I don't care, all the Jews who didn't get gassed, they moved to North London.'

The moment this experience doesn't disturb me is the moment I hang up my camera, because that must be the moment when you've become contaminated.

All the while I have to laugh and smile at this awful and painful theatre. I have to acquiesce to this, so that I won't arouse suspicion. Nothing that is in this world belongs to me or ever will. I am disgusted that I am in this position, but it confirms my conviction that Jason and his like should be exposed.

As Jason talks of war and the War, others prepare their flares and ready their fists for the night ahead. I worry about being searched while going into the ground in the company of Jason. I make arrangements on the phone with Pip to remove my ample recording kit before the game and give it to a member of the team when I can. I will have to try and sneak out at half-time and readmit myself with it on.

Jason, Paul and I get a taxi to the ground and, despite our tickets for the neutral end, get wisely directed to the away-supporters end. Jay is disappointed. Much better to ruck among the enemy is his thought.

In the company of our fat boy ('The Penguin', as his friends call him, though not to his face), a banner is unfurled: 'FUCK OFF LAUDRUP YOU CUNT GO HOME!' Brian Laudrup was playing his last game for Chelsea and would be returning the next day to play for his home team, Copenhagen [FC København] – today's opponents.

The wind is coarse and the company coarser still. Ken Bates, the Chairman of Chelsea Football Club, exhorts the police to get the banner taken down at half-time and Jason does not like it, not one little bit. The flares shoot off and in the spot-lit, smoke-filled haze The Penguin emerges, David Koresh-like, calling upon his disciples to join him. After a tug of war with the police, which Jason loses, he keeps his arms aloft and apart chanting, 'Chelsea. Chelsea. Chelsea.' The Penguin is living in glory time. This is his moment. All at home, on television, can see him now. This is what he lives for.

The final result is København 0 Chelsea 1. The winning goal is scored by Brian Laudrup. Still there is no contrition for the banner that was unleashed just twenty-five minutes before Laudrup put Chelsea into the next round.

Much later that night, when we are out celebrating Chelsea's victory, my hooligan credentials are given the ultimate seal of approval. I am beaten up by a mob of twenty shaven-headed FC København fans on the prowl and dressed to kill. There is no doubting their intentions as they approach. I have learned to sense these moments. One look in an eye, one turn of a shoulder, and you know.

In times like these you rely on instinct. Luckily and worryingly, my first instinct is journalistic. I press the disguised car-key fob that turns on my tee-shirt camera seconds before they attack. With fly-kicks and punches, they drag me onto the main street in Copenhagen and try to shoo me into the traffic. I can't distinguish what blows exactly are pouring down on me, but it's a heavy down-fall. Pushed and skewered into the gutter, I get crushed and mauled and become intimately acquainted with a bicycle stand and a few boots. 'Get off, fucking pricks, get off prick, fuck off...' It's not quite piece-to-camera material for a BBC reporter. I've obviously been hanging around football hooligans too long.

My next instinct is survival. I grab one leg of an FC København fan, reasoning that at least he can't kick with the leg I am holding and not with the other one, either, unless he wants to end up flat on his arse like me. It occurs to me that if he's in the way, too, there will be less room for others to kick my head in. I am right and eventually it dissipates.

With several pathetic bounds I am free. I can taste blood in my mouth but nothing seems to be broken. Miraculously, not even the camera. I thank God that I had turned it on. There is no point getting my head smashed in if it isn't on camera. However, my phone transmitter recorder, about £1,000-pounds-worth of equipment, disguised as a mobile, is gone. The fight isn't the only bollocking I'm going to get.

Jason, too, it transpires, had seen some action, probably from the same guys who beat me up. He describes his ruck with much bravado.

'I must have had fifteen on me, kicking me...got up and, basically, I'm on my toes.'

'You must have been steaming, mate, 'cos we were looking for you,' I say.

'Yeah, I just went home and got hold of my lot and said, "Come on, we're going to fucking work here."'

'Did you catch them? Did you see them?' I inquire.

'Well once you start, fucking any cunt was going to get it now, won't they? You know what I mean?'

And so Jason went to war and had returned to the city streets after his altercation with a mob and initiated a random purge.

6th November 1998

Hookers, hooligans and hassle. I could do without all three, given the choice. Today there is no choice. We are heading home with

Jason and he is determined to make the most of our three-hour stopover in Amsterdam. That, though, is the least of my hassles. We are at the airport and I have to get my secret camera kit through the security check and x-ray just yards from the departure gate. Paul creates a diversion, dragging Jason off to Duty Free, and I run to the security gate. I have some leeway, but I don't know just how much.

'Could you open your bag, sir?', the security man asks suspiciously. He peers inside. 'Would you mind telling me what this is?'

I am happy to oblige, but I wish he would keep his voice down. 'I am a journalist and this is a covert camera,' I say, looking for signs of Jason.

'Very interesting,' he says. 'Could I ask who you are working for and what you are investigating?'

'Yes, you can ask, but I can't tell you. I am sorry.' Not uninterested, he bids me farewell. Just as I leave him Jason comes into view. It's a close call.

We take off for Amsterdam. Jason loves his hookers and is insistent about having his carnal playtime. As soon as we land at Schipol Airport we journey to Dam Square, turn right over the canal and go into the red-light district. He chats about his fantasies and which women he will pick from the abundant window fare. Paul and I join in the conversation but defer to his expert opinion on 'whores'. Jason directs us to where all the white women occupy their window boxes. I am grateful we part to make our respective choices. While Jason has his 'choice bit of rump', Paul and I retire to a Dutch coffee house, unusually – especially for a 'drug dealer' – to have coffee. Jason returns sated and quiet, and we make our way back to Schipol, where I manage to give him the slip long enough to hand the covert camera over to Pip, thus saving me the security hassle again.

Driving home from the airport with the secret camera in the car softly whirring, I chat to Jason.

DONAL: 'Lucky to have that three-hour gap in Amsterdam. Our luck was with us there?'

[There had been some debate as to whether there would be enough time to make the flight and to get to the red-light district in the city centre.]

JASON: 'We'd have made it, man, two and a half hours, it would have been tight, a lot tighter than her,' [referring to the prostitute he had in Amsterdam].

DONAL: 'Mine was all right, though.'

JASON: '...I've got to look in every window. I went over the canal and all. I see one there and I've been fucking there before... She was shocking – shocking turnout. Her tits are like that [gestures with his hands cupped and outstretched], her nipples are like gorilla's thumbs, oh, handsome chappies.'

With that, more or less, Paul and I part company with Jason. I drop him off at his tyre business and that is the end of one tiresome and difficult adventure.

    Home. Safe.

8th November 1998

It's a day of two games: Jason's and Chelsea's. Jason is playing for a local football team in Feltham (he plays for several teams on different days of the week) and Paul and I are going to support him. Then we are going on to watch Chelsea play West Ham. This premiership game is normally a police nightmare as the enmities between the two clubs are infamous.

    Jason's team is playing an away match in Southall and we are driving him and a mate there. It makes for an interesting journey. Southall has a large Asian community and Jason is keen to let everyone know just what he thinks of the ethnic mix in this area. 'Go home you fucking monkeys, fuck off you Paki wankers,' he shouts out the window at an elderly Asian man. I am glad when we get to the ground.

On the pitch, Jason looks like some Disney cartoon figure with his silky feet and dumpy body. Despite his flab he is a bit of an artist with the ball; too slow, but assured and with good footballing vision. He is focused and in full flow, offering encouraging words for his team-mates and venom for the opposition. The sight of this roly-poly figure with his dinky footwork gets some amused encouragement from the crowd and certainly lots from me. I cheer his every move, then wonder if I have overdone it. Our relationship is not yet that comfortable that I can give him praise unreservedly. Less is more. I must remember this mantra. Colin was always on at me about it in fashion. The more you say, the more you can get into trouble.

Jason's team wins the match 3–2.

'You had a good game out there, Jay,' I compliment him.

'Yeah, it was all right. Nice bit of space out there, so you can fucking knock the ball about a bit.'

Everybody likes talking about their game. For my job, it's best to be a listener, though I am naturally a talker. This shared interest may be the quickest way into Jason's psyche. I continue to butter him up. I spread it on thick.

'Nobody's got that skill. You create space.'

'Well, if you've got a brain, you can find yourself [space], the little holes. You can read the game and read the ball coming to you eventually.' He is very proud of his game and his deft touches. My line is yielding results. He is warming to me.

'You were the only thinking man on the pitch,' I say.

'Obviously, when you watch, it looks better.'

'You made idiots of them.'

'You don't appreciate it yourself when you are on the pitch.'

Flattery is a wonderful tool. 'I just fucking thought, I set up all three, didn't I? I hadn't thought of that,' Jason reminds me happily. He continues to shout abuse from the car. 'Fuck off, you black cunt. I've had enough of you lot around today.'

Attention turns to the big game this afternoon. Chelsea and West Ham are old rivals and the scar runs deep between them. Our inside information is that there is going to be trouble – it is going to 'kick off', as they say. We have a contact who feeds information along the food chain, allowing us to sometimes get such advance information. The problem with these Chinese whispers is that often they get lost in translation, meaning that our orchestrated and intricate plots come to nothing.

Driving to the game, I didn't get the impression from Jason that violence of the organized type was on the agenda. He was too busy shouting further racist abuse at the residents of Southall. Jason is 100 per cent racist and 110 per cent Chelsea. He eats and sleeps Chelsea. He tells me that, when he goes to bed with a woman, he'll ask her to wear the Chelsea kit.

'You gotta, ain't ya? Put on a fucking old pair of shorts, pull them to one side – waay haaay!' he says. As he is coming, he shouts, 'Come on, Chels, come on Chels'.

The game passes without incident, ending in a one-all draw. There may be a reason why there is no action today. It relates to an incident in a pub in Reading two years ago, when a West Ham fan ended up with 300 stitches after being slashed across the throat in an organized fight with the Chelsea mob. It went to court, but the victim didn't give evidence and the case was dropped. Jason recounts this to us, ending up, 'We have some proper hatred between us at the moment, after that Reading thing, so I wouldn't do nothing.'

I give Jason and his friend a lift home and put music on in the car. Everyone is tired. Jason is not in the mood to talk, so I turn the camera in the car off. He is tired just being Jason. I am tired being me and everyone else.

9th November 1998

My nails have never looked less appealing. I mean that they have never looked so ugly – they're always appealing to me. I don't know why I nibble my nails rather than smoke, but it's a habit that seems equally hard to break. I have taken a leave of absence from Stop 'n'

Grow – I am beginning to like the taste of the nail poison. For the moment I will let my nails disappear under the stress. For the moment I have too much else to worry about.

10th November 1998

Decisions are being made on the care-home story. We are considering one home in particular. While I am role-playing as a hooligan, we are going to send Lee, our team researcher, in to work at the home for a short time to confirm the substance of the allegations that we have heard. Initially he will not be filming or recording, just gather-ing information. It is not hard to get a job as a care assistant. The pay is bad and the hours anti-social, so there is usually a high turnover of staff. I am sure Lee will have no problem.

12th November 1998

I get as far as Dublin, in an attempt to have a brief holiday and see family, when I am called back. My plan to chill out and forget all about football is rudely interrupted. Jason needs me. Nonetheless I get to meet my five-year-old nephew. When I see him, he always asks me to tell him stories with the same ingredients: three bits of danger, a monster and a big journey. Oh, I thought, sounds a bit like a channel Controller – he'll be asking for audience figures next.

14th November 1998

I am feeling sorry for myself. I should be in Ireland. I am tired and red-cheeked and irritable. Worse, I am sloppy on the job. Chelsea are playing Wimbledon today, my real team. I've got to go and cheer for the opposition and my heart isn't in it. Instead of meeting up with a load of hooligans before the match, I persuade Paul to go for coffee instead. I feel I need some space. I wonder if I have taken on too much.

We go to the game. I can't see Jason around, but his car is

parked up. I join in the Chelsea chants in lacklustre fashion. Wimbledon is losing. More than any other time I feel I do not belong. Chelsea wins, 3–0. It isn't too difficult to track down Jason after the match. Where there is fried chicken, Jason is never far away. I go to the takeaway on Fulham Broadway and wait.

Jason is sweet after the game. He is dressed like a Parisian, with a beret and long trench coat. He doesn't often dress like this, but occasionally he will dress incongruously for a hooligan. I remember then that he borrowed the beret and trench coat to cover the mud on his clothes after his street fights in Copenhagen. To see him walk down the Fulham Road is amazing. Everyone knows him and holds him up for a chat.

'All right, Jay?', people shout across the street.

'Yeah, cushty, mate,' he returns with a boyish grin. Next thing he'll be kissing babies. This walk from the stadium to his car is his dignity, his village. This is respect time. He takes it in like a sponge. By the time he gets to me, he's sweeter with me than ever.

'All right, Macca?'

'Yeah, sweet, mate. Good result, eh?'

He holds court as usual. He is more comfortable with me than he has ever been, though there is still a little bit of reserve. I ask him about his own game and he tells me to come and watch him play. In fact, he repeats it three times. I guess that he *really* wants me there.

I say casually, 'If I'm not keeping busy with work 'n' all, I'll wander down, mate.' Less is more.

15th November 1998

I go to Feltham to watch Jason play and stand on the sideline in the mud. My cheeks are red, raw from the chaffing cold and driving wind. It's the kind of weather that requires commitment.

I arrive before half-time. It's enough to make my presence felt. Another little nudge for Jason, building up a picture of me and my relationship with him. Like any friendship, we're learning more about each other as we go along. What I'm learning about him is helping me to inveigle my way more effectively into his life. What he's finding out about me is stuff he understands and appreciates.

Jason thinks I'm a serious player, a drug dealer who brings in high-grade 'skunk' from the West Indies. He also believes I'm an Orangeman and that I've lost a brother to the IRA. It's a picture that's been carefully constructed to appeal to his prejudices and hates. And his loves. He thinks I rate Chelsea as highly as he does. He thinks I'm so mad about football that I even like to watch him play in the freezing cold for the Chiswick and District league. That's what Jason thinks.

I leave at the end of the game without talking to the man himself. I don't have to speak to him to move our relationship on. What is unsaid is more important than what is. Unlike most journalists, criminals and hooligans are very economical with their language but, unlike most journalists, verbose with their violence.

16th November 1998

We have discussed it long and hard and agreed: I have to have a tattoo. I thought it might come to this, but I still can't believe I'm going to do it.

I don't really have a choice. It's part of the uniform. Going undercover is all about talking the talk, walking the walk and wearing the kit. I can chant the chants and I've got the garb – the Nike hat, the Stone Island jacket and the Reebok trainers – but I haven't got a tattoo, the definitive badge of a hooligan.

I will have by tomorrow, though. Tonight we drive up to Manchester (I can't do it in London because of security concerns). Tomorrow I go to a Manchester tattoo parlour.

17th November 1998

Who am I today? For part of the day I am Mike, a kindly transient applying for a job as a care-worker. Lee should be in the care home by early December and I am to follow suit. I am calling today to organize a job interview. His trip into the first care home will indicate whether there is cause for concern in this sector. He will pursue the investigation in the home and I will gauge his experience to build up a clear picture of the care industry and the particular company running the home.

For another part of the day I am Macca, the football hooligan. Macca goes to a tattoo parlour to get his obsession with Chelsea carved indelibly into his flesh. Hiding behind Macca's machismo is me. Violent, penetrative self-mutilation is not quite my thing.

I do not expect the pain. It's a dull, unremitting pain that goes deeper than my skin, piercing to the heart of my psyche. There's probably no one among my family and friends with a tattoo. Until now. I hadn't realized what threshold I was crossing until I was on the other side. I grimace and grin, not caring whether the camera is rolling. (Outside the football context I can be filmed openly.) I make the mistake of glancing down at my arm before the tattooist has finished his artwork. My eyes roll over and turn back. The grin goes. So does the grimace. Fear and faintness overwhelm me and I lose face. The room blurs and everything around me starts to dissolve. I become a thin filament of plastic, stretched too tight and starting to tear. I roll my body forward.

The tattoo artist says to the crew, pointing to me, 'He's not feeling too well, this guy.'

I echo, 'No, I'm not feeling too well.'

He tells me to lean forward and to put my head between my legs. While I am semiconscious, he talks to me and puts me at ease. In the same position he continues to drill into my arm and complete the badge and my identity.

I have never felt these feelings before, at least not all together. The closest experience to it was almost drowning when I capsized my canoe and got stuck in my boat. Having the tattoo done is worse, much worse than the act of drowning. Take my word for it.

I eventually recover my colour, my whereabouts and feel

human again. I survive. There are a few more lives left. But mine will never be the same again. I can laser off the artistry, but not the experience.

The uniform is complete. I am Macca, the football thug.

19th November 1998

R vs Moonesinghe and Others
Operation Kitson
'I am writing to advise you that the above case is due to be committed for trial at Southwark Crown Court, 1 English Grounds, Battle Bridge Lane, London SE1 2HU, to be held within the next twelve months. Most witnesses who have made statements will be required to attend Court and give evidence...'

The Crown Prosection Service has contacted me at the BBC offices. A film I did with *World In Action* last year is resulting in a number of prosecutions. A small gang headed by a Sri Lankan solicitor was running a bogus weddings racket and selling brides and grooms for up to £5,000 for immigration purposes. Some of the women had been 'married' over twenty times. I lived in a crack house with several drug addicts, some of whom were playing the role of adoring bride to feed their habit. One man – Moonesinghe, the ringleader – has been extradited from Canada to face trial. I am due to be the main witness. The court case could last up to three weeks and I can expect to be in the dock for at least a week. I'll have to have a talk with Granada, the BBC lawyers and the CPS because there may be security issues at stake here. Press coverage of that case may blow my cover in any of the worlds I hope to be operating in next spring.

Paul, my hooligan friend, is working hard and it is taking its toll. He doesn't look well today. He has a chronic pain in his chest. He shies away from the suggestion of a doctor and ploughs on regardless. 'No time for pain,' he says.

20th November 1998

Con men are on my mind. Solomon has been in contact. He asks not to be forgotten. He is not. We will get together shortly to discuss the next stage in the scam. We now have our very own mark prepared for delivery to Solomon. He is retired Detective Superintendent Peter Coles. He has investigated these frauds as a policeman and is going to be my guide in our elaborate ruse to sting the con men. We are aware that we need to build up more evidence of Peter's lottery win to show the 419 fraudsters. Peter suggests that we create a newspaper headline and front page, with appropriate photographs showing his apparent winning moment with the lottery cheque and champagne. We organize a meeting with Solomon for the end of the month. There he will give me a more refined map of our 'joint enterprise' to take Peter's alleged winnings off him. I will bring Solomon up to date on Peter's movements and get his reaction to the initial seeds which were supposedly sown at the first meeting.

21st November 1998

This day has been a long time coming. Now, at last, it seems as if all the months spent cajoling, anticipating, caressing and tickling the belly of the beast may finally pay off. I am travelling to an away game – Chelsea vs Leicester – with Jason. Our intelligence is that there might be organized violence. Jason has already intimated as much.

Paul and I are due to meet Jason at his garage in Feltham at 9.00a.m. On the really dangerous assignments, company is required for safety purposes. If you are found out and exposed – just suppose a loose wire is spotted – there is no knowing what a mob of hooligans will do to you, especially if you are alone. And this could be a very dangerous assignment. I have a gut feeling about this.

The reason, I think, is because Jason asked the other day if there would be just the three of us in the car. The plan was for Paul, Jason and me – and no one else – to travel up. I don't know why he asked the question but it stuck in my mind and made me slightly nervous.

That was a few days ago, and the feeling hasn't gone away. It's got worse. Today I am frightened. These instincts are sharp now. I pull up to the garage and obsessively check the car to make sure nothing has been left in the pockets or the ashtray that might betray my real life, or indeed another bogus one. All is well. Then Jason's blue Vauxhall Vectra pulls up. There are three men in it. 'Here he is,' I say to Paul.

'And he's got someone with him,' Paul adds.

He blanches as he recognizes a face. 'It's Andy Frain,' he says.

'Fuck,' I say, voice quivering. The name is familiar to me. I have seen it on hooligan photofits. It's an imposing face and I recognize it without difficulty. He is dangerous and described by some sources as capable of the most irrational violence. He knows no limits and acts violently by instinct and without a thought or care to the consequences. He was a National Front candidate for Feltham, where Jason now lives, and has more than fifty assorted convictions. His nickname is 'Nightmare'.

I think about the advice Paul gave me as we pulled up. 'Less is more. Let's be excited. Nice, low-key start.'

I say, 'That's right. You're fucking right [getting in the mood]. That's what I'll do. No language, sorry, mate, you're right. No bad language.'

Paul replies, 'Using bad language is not a problem, but using the *wrong* bad language is a problem.' We have to be so careful: a misplaced word could have us killed. That is no exaggeration. The threat shows in my face and Paul's, but only we detect it.

Suddenly, I remember when I had most recently heard the nickname Nightmare. He was the guy who went with Jason to Auschwitz and urinated on the grave. I can't believe it. I try not to panic, but all I can think is, Oh God, he will be sitting just a foot away from me. I will be new to him and I will be under his scrutiny for more than three hours, maybe more. Paul and I are both smoking. No cigarette in history has a harder pull on it than the moment after I see Nightmare's face. I nearly sucked mine into my mouth.

We have been wrong-footed. Things could go horribly wrong.

I rush back to the car where Paul has left some blank tapes in the elasticated pocket at the back of the front seat. We left them there because we thought we could put Jason in front. Now it's all change. I frantically take out the tapes and spare recording disks and place them in the driver's pocket. I throw a cigatrette packet over them. They are hidden – for now.

'They are both coming up with us. That's Andy Frain,' Paul confirms, eyes pointing in the direction ahead. There is little more than nervous laughter coming from my mouth.

Eventually there is no choice. I have to be ready. 'OK, let's go. Are you getting in the front or the back?'

'I think I should sit in the front,' Paul says. The previous plan, to put Jason in the front, would have allowed a carefully positioned camera to get him in the centre frame. That plan *was* a good one. I suggest that Paul sits in the front for the first part of the journey, so that we can move Jason into the hot seat later for pictures. With a wry smile and amid some tension, Paul says, 'I think I should sit in the front for the whole thing. We need a bit of comfort zone here.' I laugh at the thought.

The boys load into the car. Jason and Andy are accompanied by another hooligan, Ian Payne. The three line the back seat with Andy on the throne in the middle holding court. Introductions are made.

I deliver a handshake to Andy like an Exocet and squeeze robust and firm all the way through.

'All right, mate.' I hold his eye just a little longer than normal as a trust-building exercise. I remember that Jason had said to me last week, 'I can't be doing with those black man's slap and high-five, whoop and holler 'n' shit. I hate them fuckin' wankers. Me, I like a good English handshake, a man's handshake.' And so I am overcompensating. Andy's hand is smaller than mine and he has a firm and measured grip, the grip of a man who is not too sure of the man whose hand he is sharing.

I drive off, knowing – but not much reassured – that there will be a car filming my car, as well as another van with a second crew, and two other BBC journalists rigged up with secret cameras. They'll be on call, just in case. In addition to all this I have got a tee-shirt camera on and I have a camera rigged up in the car. Paul, too, is wearing a covert rig.

It's not long before Jason and his pals start chatting in the back. The talk is of the passport restrictions that the police put on foot-ball hooligans after the World Cup. 'They took mine away. I still had to sign on when fucking England were playing abroad. I didn't even have a fucking passport and I still had to go to the police station,' Andy complains.

He starts to joke about police press conferences in which he and his friends have been alluded to. In full variety performance he acts out the role of the senior police officer, putting on a mocking PC Plod voice: 'He's [speaking about Andy] the brains behind the outfit... We've arrested them many times but they keep escaping our clutches.' I have a stand-up comic sitting down in the back seat. He is funny, but there is no hiding the menace that lies behind his sharp eyes.

Andy continues, talking about himself in the voice of a police-man. 'They dress in suits and... like to go to a pub, start a bit of action, and then sit back and watch it happen.' His lips contort to enhance the insulting caricature. 'They're so highly praised by their moronic followers, all they have to do is shout the word and they steam into battle for them.' He says that he read the report of the press conference in the *Star* – it was headlined, 'JET SET SICKOS' and his mates were buying him drinks to celebrate.

Nonetheless, Andy is clearly proud of his notoriety. He boasts that the police described him as 'brutal'. Mimicking the policeman again, he says, 'He can fix anything from a bar-room brawl to an international riot... This man's ruthless, won't stop at anything, £50,000 robberies and all that violence.'

Jason laughs. 'Seem to know you quite well.'

I laugh, too, for appearances and for my own safety. Is this a not-so-subtle warning to us, I wonder? Andy reveals that he has spent nine of the past thirteen years in jail. He is certainly laying his credentials on the line. The conversation continues. Sometimes I guess I am expected to nod and laugh and at other times I am supposed to be disinterested. This is one conversation I have to acquiesce to.

ANDY: 'Black cunts! Do we like niggers? NO! We hate
          niggers. In fact we hate any cunt who ain't British.
          I hate Frogs. Frogs wind me up just as much.'
JASON: 'Krauts. Like their political views. Don't like them.'
          [A reference to the hooligans' strong neo-Nazi
          connections.]
ANDY: 'Tell you what annoys me as well. Reading seems
          to be the fucking dumping ground for all them
          fucking Bosnians and that. Every afternoon, they
          get about five or six of them out from the back of
          a lorry. I'll have to get the boys out on the streets.'

We're about half-way to Leicester on the M1 and there is sweat dripping down my face. I am wiping furiously to hide it. Meanwhile, whenever the boys say anything compromising, I try to turn on the camera that is staring out from the dashboard. There is an on and off button, but I can't look while Andy is so close, so I do it by touch and hope that my improvized Braille technique works.

Amid all the banter the telephone calls come and go as they discuss arrangements for rioting later on. 'Hello, mate, Nightmare here,' Andy answers. He gets off the phone. There are three coaches on the way, all up for action. He repeats the conversation he had with one of his mates on one of the buses. His mate was left on the bus while other Chelsea fans are on the rampage in Hemel Hempstead en route to the game. 'He said "we're up to full strength" and the boys are "swigging beer, snorting Charlie [cocaine] and eating sandwiches".'

There is excitement brewing in the back. And then!

'Today's the day,' Jason says.

Above left: My disguise as a hooligan at the World Cup is working too well. I try to persuade the authorities that looks can be deceiving.
Above: Suffering from frostbite, I emerge after eighteen hours' canoeing, days before I go undercover.
Left: My idiot's guide to photography helped me look like a photographer, but tragically failed to turn me into one.
Below: Putting on my recording equipment, often in the unlikeliest places. After a year of being a lager-drinking hooligan, I put on so much weight the gear didn't fit.

Above: Carlisle's *News & Star* offers us a mock-up style of its front page to help convince Solomon that our story about having access to a lottery winner is true.
Right: Our pretend lottery winner receives his fake cheque from Derek Hatton, who helps us out on our scam to sting the '419'ers.

Above: Far-right activists attack a 'Bloody Sunday' commemoration march. I lag behind. Andy 'Nightmare' Frain leads the charge.
Below left: Jason emerges from the red plumes of smoke, cheering on his beloved Chelsea in Copenhagen. After the game, he went off to beat up some locals.
Below right: After being searched by the police, a BBC TV crew try to film me. Perhaps the hooligan in me protests too much.

Right: Oliver (left) and Diego (right), two members of Milan's most famous group of PRs, the Moonsinners, celebrate London Fashion Week outside the McQueen show.

Middle: Probably the worst photograph ever taken of Naomi Campbell (at the Gianfranco Ferré show in Milan). A very proud moment.

Below left: The night I first meet one of Elite's (the model agency) top bosses, Gérald Marie, in Milan. Later, he took prostitutes back to his hotel and ordered extra condoms from the porter.

Below right: I destroy some high-grade Brazilian cocaine given to me by one of the PRs. I flush it down the toilet in a high-grade hotel in Milan.

Above: I watch Jason play football, heaping praise from the sideline. Initially he is uncomfortable with it, but soon soaks it up. His socks hide the words: 'When we're good, they never remember, when we're bad, they never forget'.
Below: This shot of Jason and me is caught by a concealed camera in the car. Jason looks nervous – I'm a terrible driver.

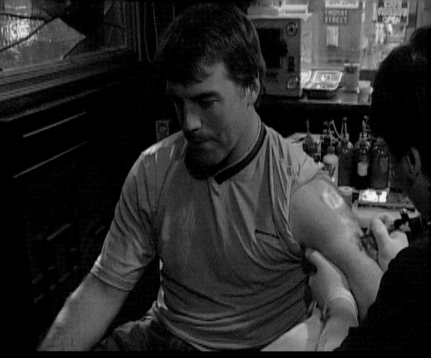

Above: The tattoo is part of the hooligan's uniform and, if I want to survive, I have to get one. I didn't expect to collapse with the pain.
Below: Solomon (right) and his bodyguard meet me in a hotel lobby. I tell him that I am looking for a 'cherry picker' and that he is the best around.

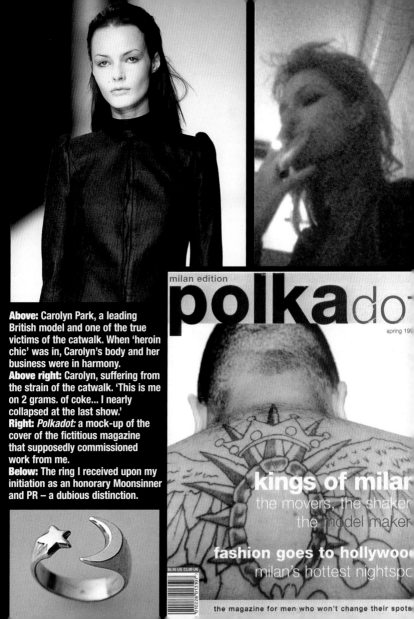

Above: Carolyn Park, a leading British model and one of the true victims of the catwalk. When 'heroin chic' was in, Carolyn's body and her business were in harmony.
Above right: Carolyn, suffering from the strain of the catwalk. 'This is me on 2 grams. of coke... I nearly collapsed at the last show.'
Right: *Polkadot:* a mock-up of the cover of the fictitious magazine that supposedly commissioned work from me.
Below: The ring I received upon my initiation as an honorary Moonsinner and PR – a dubious distinction.

milan edition

polkadot

spring 199

kings of milan
the movers, the shaker
the model maker

fashion goes to hollywoo
milan's hottest nightspo

$6.95 US £3.00 UK

the magazine for men who won't change their spots

Above: Andy 'Nightmare' Frain (in white shirt) admits to stabbing a policeman. He is a Chelsea Head-hunter and former member of the Ku Klux Klan.

Left: Solomon (far left) and I discuss how we should work together to defraud the spoof lottery winner I have provided: former Detective Super-intendent Peter Coles.

Right: I took this photograph of the girls lining up for the Moscow final of the Elite Model Look Competition, at Gérald Marie's invitation. The international event attracts up to 350,000 entries from nearly sixty countries.

Andy smirks. 'And you've brought the new recruits out.'

In a twinkling, we are anointed. I tell myself to hang on in there and make no mistakes. For the moment, anyway, it feels just a little bit safer – until our precarious situation is reinforced by Nightmare boasting that he stabbed an off-duty policeman. If he is capable of that, then he is truly capable of anything.

'He had his throat proper cut,' Jason says.

Andy takes up the story. 'We was laughing at him, we was. He [the policeman] says, "You can't do that, I'm an off-duty police-man." I said, SHUT UP [he roars]. It's one o'clock in the morning – nobody can see us [he makes a slashing motion]. His bird ran off hysterical, we was just laughing...' Nightmare's voice travels like a rollercoaster loop, as melodic as it is malicious. I laugh when he laughs and smile appreciatively at all the appropriate moments. It does not make me feel any safer. There is the scent of threat in the air. Nightmare was never pulled in for that attack, but he was arrest-ed when he and other fans were found to have a massive armoury in their van. The police found a rocket launcher and guns, he says.

This is fascinating. We are getting right to the heart of football violence and its terror and organization. This is what we came into this sphere to show, but I have mixed emotions. Journalistically we have gained access to a closed world, but there is a dangerous and vile hooligan in the back seat. There is little time for reflection. I only hope that the cameras are working. You can never tell until you come out of the field. Andy is now talking about a pre-arranged confrontation between the Head-hunters and 200 of Hibernian's City Service Squad, a hooligan squad. 'We were on the phone – we're coming, you motherfuckers.' This is the way the violence is organized. It is planned in advance with phone calls between the two sides, who agree on the rules of engagement. In this particular instance, the police got wind of it and arrested everyone within sight. Nightmare – who had a pocketful of Ku Klux Klan cards on him (he used to be a member of the Windsor Chapter of the KKK) – was not charged with the attack.

The closer we get to Leicester, the more excited the guys become. More phone calls are made and it transpires the Leicester boys had agreed to organize a ruck in Narborough, a small village not far from Leicester. The meet has been rearranged to avoid police attention. Nightmare's hands are sweating in anticipation. 'That's enough now. Marquis of Queensbury. Let's get it on!' he shouts. Jason exclaims that he is 'Man United-excited!'.

We arrive at the Narborough Arms and there are three coaches outside. Inside, it is packed with Chelsea fans. I recognize a few faces from Copenhagen. I hope they might recognize me, too, and remember my association with Jason. I buy Andy/Nightmare a drink and then withdraw, keen not to be too much in their faces.

Within minutes, vanloads of police surround the pub and encircle the village. They must have had inside information – just like us. The fight is quashed before it even has a chance to get started. The police make clear their intentions to follow the fans to the game. After that, Jason decides to board the bus rather than continuing in our car because, he says, 'I don't want to bring the Old Bill down on your car, mate.' There will be no trouble before the game. Andy stays in the pub with Ian. They may be staying up the whole weekend. I say goodbye and promise to link up with Jason on the phone after the game.

Paul and I drive off. For the first time in nearly four hours we get a chance to relax. We exhale deeply. I feel as if I have just jumped out of the path of an avalanche and am watching it thunder past, unscathed. I need to do something to strip myself of the experience, so I take off my Ralph Lauren sweatshirt with the circuitboard lens and unstrap the recorder and the microphones that are wrapped around my body. There is sticky tape against my chest. I grimace and shriek as I tear it off, hair and all. I need to be free of it all. Just for an hour.

We retreat to an indoor bowling club for a cup of coffee and a roll.

After the game, I try to park the car near the ground before contacting Jason. For about ten minutes Paul and I have a workers' tiff, nit-picking over this and that and generally being irritable with each other. We have the sense to realize it is a symptom of the extreme stress we are under and manage to laugh ourselves out of it.

Radio Five Live interrupts this happy catharsis with news about trouble outside the ground. David Mellor, the radio presenter and football pundit, introduces a distressed fan who describes the scenes of violence he has witnessed. He tells the story of a friend, a family man with a small child, who, despite the police's best efforts at seg-regating the opposing fans, found himself and his kid caught up in a battle between Leicester and Chelsea thugs.

I ring Jason again.

'I've been a bit busy, mate, on my toes. I'm taking the train home, mate, give me a bell tomorrow. See ya, mate.' Which translates as: There has been some fighting and Jason has left on the train.

The fan continues relating the trauma he witnessed. He says that there were about twenty in the group of Chelsea fans shouting and goading and punching and kicking indiscriminately. He saw a man walking with his little boy who'd been punched. The child went home and put down his scarf and told his mother that he never wanted to go to football again. He was only seven years of age.

For one listener and one fan, today is the day that football died.

Score: Leicester 2 Chelsea 4.

25th November 1998

The photographs from the mad three weeks of fashion have come back to fester. I pray that one or two photographs will offer some potential, but for the most part they range from really bad to down-right awful. I am just grateful that the camera was turned on; that was a task in itself. It's one thing playing a photographer – that I think I managed rather well – and quite another thing being one. I have never pretended I could do the business, but inside I'm a tiny bit disappointed. It's easy to be seduced by the photographer's get-up and garb. I have always thought it to be a sexy occupation, though I suspect that, had I ever become one, I would never have found myself in the privileged position of propositioning Naomi for just one turn for the lens. There are not many photographers who can make her look fat and dumpy. Now that takes real talent.

The fashion story doesn't end with the photographs. I now have to build on my relationships with the PRs and others in the business. I will continue to flounder hopelessly as a photographer, but the catwalk work doesn't come around until the spring. Now that I am known as a photographer I don't have to take any pictures, but I will use my exhibition as a tool to get closer to some of the characters I've already met. There will be more trips to Milan and Paris in the offing before Christmas if I can fit it in with the rest of the lives. It's getting pretty busy now.

I am due for an interview in a few days' time at the care home and that will turn my schedule from plain busy to plain mad. I have to learn my CV and prepare for it. There is no point falling at the first hurdle.

27th November 1998

New initiatives against football violence have been announced. I attend the press conference at the Arsenal football ground in Highbury, but I do not want to be caught on camera in a random cutaway by another crew. It would not do for my Chelsea mates to see me on the evening news fraternizing with the enemy. I stand at the back and keep my head down.

The politicians are genuinely trying to do their best against hooliganism. Tony Banks, the sports minister, says something amazingly prescient. 'Football hooligans could be anybody, look like anyone, they could look like you or I.' I think, you ain't half right there, my son.

Later in the afternoon, we have a strategy meeting about the fraud investigation. Things are moving on and phone calls have been exchanged. We are another step closer to ensnaring our quarry. The Nigerian con men think the same. A meeting is set for tomorrow to discuss the 'business opportunity' I have previously aired with Solomon.

28th November 1998

Today I am a bodyguard to a lottery winner again. Solomon is aware of my history, the history that I want him to know. My bogus history has me down as having a military background (former SAS) and depicts me as cool and ruthless. I have now got to live the role as before. I am stern, but not as stoic and efficiently spoken as Macca the hooligan. No one could speak quite as fast as Mac the photographer and I am not sure how fast Mike the care worker speaks. He is waiting in the wings. I dread to ask anyone just how much the real Donal talks.

I am due to meet Solomon at noon in Chiswick to move the scam along. Our plan is for an outside hit to allow our photographer to get long-lens shots, but the weather has intervened. Our team has a 9.30a.m. command meeting at the BBC offices in White City. This has the feel of a big operation, but not quite the stress. After spending five hours in the company of a knife-wielding maniac, the other investigations seem easy.

Solomon is late. Very late. I discuss with the team whether to be angry and just how angry I should be. The consensus is to be annoyed but not so annoyed as to cause offence. It is a thin line. When Solomon arrives, he is accompanied by two others, one wearing a bow tie and one dressed in jeans and a jacket. This is unexpected. I think back to last week's surprise and decide it couldn't be that bad and put all fears out of my head. I tap my watch and admonish. Solomon, dressed resplendently, acknowledges his time-keeping *faux pas* and blames the traffic.

Once again, we have all the cameras out for this one. Our photographer is taking discreet pictures from a car 40 metres away and there are secret cameras, including one woven tightly around my chest and a camera concealed in a van on the street. I am overloaded with equipment. I have a radio transmitter ariel in my right armpit. There is a mini-disc microphone going from my chest through my boxers (no indignity spared) into the machine in my left pocket and a digital recorder, controller and batteries strapped to my body and taped down with gaffer tape. There is also the transmitter in my mobile phone.

The Nigerians fill in the details of the scam. It is audacious and incredibly well choreographed. Every move and counter-move is prepared for. Fictitious names, documents – nothing is left to chance. It is a remarkable operation, but not quite as remarkable as they think. This time Solomon is not stoned. He is more loquacious and stutters a lot less. Must have been the drugs. We are both more comfortable with each other. His bodyguard starts taking interest in a game of draughts that is being played on a nearby table.

He invites himself to the table to play a game. Both the players, Lee and Mike, work for the team and are filming the meeting. This unsolicited invitation takes us unawares, but Mike doesn't flinch one bit and proceeds to beat him convincingly.

I think I am doing well, but I don't notice that in fact I am being careless, smoking and spilling more ash than Vesuvius, and not just on me but on Solomon's expensive tailored clothes.

My smoking notwithstanding, the hit is a success. The next step is to introduce the mark (Peter) to the Nigerians. That is the important meeting, the one which will persuade them to take me and my mark seriously. There is a thought that this meeting might take place in Amsterdam, but Solomon says he will get back to me on the details.

After the meeting, I undress. This involves tearing reams of tape – which keeps my covert kit secure – off my body and hairy chest. It is painful and irritates my skin, but I refuse to shave my chest for the job. It's too much to ask.

29th November 1998

My lives are getting busier now, alternating day by day and, sometimes, hour by hour. This morning I'm on call for a quick trip to Milan for a fashion show, passport at the ready. By 3.00p.m., though, the trip to Milan is postponed until Tuesday through to Friday of the following week. It's a relief because Monday and Tuesday this week I am working on the care story (the interview), Wednesday and Thursday I may be in Amsterdam for the fraud story and on Friday I am going to be a football hooligan. The weekend is up for grabs between my various roles, or I may just be myself. It is hard to juggle this psychologically and there are practical problems such as wardrobes and phone calls. I have to answer my phone in a very neutral fashion because it could be someone calling from any particular field or it could be a personal call. It just isn't practical to have a phone for each story and a fifth for my personal life. I have enough technology and gamma rays running around my body as it is. I have not got the worlds mixed up yet, but going from fashion and its cheek-to-cheek greetings to the sturdy handshakes and bad language of football can be a little unnerving.

It is totally exhausting to live like this. Tiredness is the bane of my life. I crave sleep as the crack addicts I lived with last year craved every snort and hit. I may be exaggerating.

1st December 1998

I can't believe I have been in the field so long. It's been eight months now and there's still a way to go on all the investigations. Today, I arrange my Christmas – in care. With having to juggle football seasons and fashion seasons, Christmas is the only time I can spend a few weeks together in one place. There is no telling what to expect. It promises to be as challenging as any Head-hunter journey but for altogether different reasons.

I arrive for my interview. The home is a grey building set against a grey sky, with woodchip-matted interior walls. After months of research, meetings and work on the ground, I finally push my finger on the bell. A stylish and matronly manager conducts me along narrow corridors, which have the institutional smell of an old hospital. I am wearing my secret camera under my clothes, but see no hint of the concerns over staff behaviour witnessed by our researcher who had done a short stint there before my arrival. I have no wish to witness them. I may not have a choice over my working holiday.

I present myself as a calm worker. The interview is short. The manager of the home gives me some good news. She says that they would be mad not to employ somebody like me. I am reminded that there is a massive staff shortage in this industry and this is why I look so inviting. We discuss dates and it looks like I start working the week before Christmas. I am taken around the home for a tour. It seems to have gone well. I don't know whether to look forward to Christmas or not.

2nd December 1998

It is time to progress our fraud investigation. Solomon has phoned. He is in town, but he is busy. We are keen to make arrangements for a meeting with our supposed lottery winner, Peter, and the equally fictitious son of the late President Mobutu, Solomon's very own imaginative creation. This is supposed to be the first stage in convincing the mark (Peter) that he can trust the people he is about to do business with. However, it owes much more to theatre and showmanship than trust across cultural frontiers. Truly, it looks to me like the high farce of a West End stage show. Solomon is going to appear in full African regalia, dressed up as the son of the late President Mobutu. He invites me to discuss the details at his home. I agree. This is, I reflect a bit unwise and dangerous, but I go ahead nonetheless.

I travel to Wembley with a colleague to meet Solomon at

9.00p.m. as arranged. It is a normal suburban pad and designed to allow him to keep a low profile. He is late again. One of his associates (a bodyguard from the previous meeting) lets us in and phones Solomon to check on his whereabouts. It appears he is en route. He has been in a central London hotel, relieving some poor soul of his money and, as always, business comes first.

Eventually, Solomon arrives. He unfurls a joint. The conversation unfurls, too. I give him the details of the hotel that Peter has booked into and we discuss timings. All the while I keep an eye out for guns. I can see that he is looking at me, too. Suddenly, he appears nervous. He starts to stare fixedly at the centre of my tee-shirt. Either he has simply intuited with his cat's-whisker sensitivity that something isn't right, or he is suspicious of my well-padded chest. Does he think I have a gun? I don't know, but the moment passes, the drugs take over and after a few more puffs he is at ease again. At least, he seems so to me. We finalize arrangements for the morrow. For Solomon, it's another day, another mark. I leave unsure of our relationship, but hopeful that he will deliver himself and the son of President Mobutu tomorrow.

3rd December 1998

I am going to try and tempt Jason with a Big Mac and fries. The intention is to lure him to the car park at a McDonald's not far from where he works and get him to relay his experience in Leicester, this time with good picture quality and sound. To this end we have a black van with blacked out windows already parked up, containing Pip, a sound man and a cameraman.

I give Jason a call and arrange to meet him there. Paul and I wait in the Mercedes. The van is about 30 metres away, parked so as to get a clean shot of the bonnet of our car. I am wearing a radio mike but no secret camera. It is odd to be without it. 'I feel this is like a phantom pregnancy,' I joke.

Suddenly, Paul shouts, 'Just get out, get out!' Jason has arrived.

I rush to the filming location – otherwise known as the bonnet – and lean against it casually. Although it is not warm I am wearing a tee-shirt. The sleeve on my left arm has ridden up, revealing my tattoo. This is deliberate.

We greet each other. He asks me what I've been up to. For some reason I lose my senses.

'I've just been filmmmm–' I don't quite finish the word and rush out some expletives to hide my gaff. He doesn't quite hear my mistake and instead gives the tattoo a glance and a touch.

'When did you get the Chelsea tattoo done?' The question is considered and thoughtful.

'Years ago, mate,' I say. I see satisfaction and relief in his face. I can almost see him mouth the words, 'Proper Chelsea, proper Chels'. Thank God the tattoo is paying dividends. It would have killed me if all that pain was for nothing.

The chat moves to the violence at Leicester. Jason is wearing a woollen hat with the St George's cross on it. He is a bit worried, but continues to talk. His head keeps turning to the black van. At one stage he pauses and looks at it directly and holds his gaze.

'Oh, it went fucking berserk,' he says. 'It was [happenin]g left, right and centre. It was happening, know what I mean?' He is being a bit coy because he may be worried about the van. Nonetheless, he tells me about some mates of his fellow Chelsea Head-hunters who are in court for football violence as a result. Jason, too, was involved but was not arrested. 'They had me bang to rights as well, but only nicked the people who were holding tools... a couple of top boys there didn't get nicked as well because we was just having it... If they was to nick every single one, that would mean they'd nick 150 people.

'I ain't the main man, though I'm one of them, I know every cunt... I know Man United's top geezer and I know Man City's top geezer, really well, good pals of mine, very, very good friends.'

Jason is still discernibly twitchy. I, too, am nervous because I can see him still looking at the van. I am trying to distract him by moving the conversation on to his football. He is happier. I suggest that I may and go and see him play on Sunday. We part. 'Keep active chaps, keep your heads down,' is his salutation. He, I'm sure, is glad to leave the black van behind. So, in truth, am I.

I return home dressed as a football hooligan and leave again shortly afterwards, a well-dressed man in a suit, pristine black shoes, cuff links, and an ear piece, giving every appearance of a bodyguard. What must the neighbours think, I wonder.

Today, Peter, our mark, is supposed to meet 'the late Prince Mobutu's son', who is going to ask him for help to remove millions of dollars from Ghana where it is now apparently in a vault. After the meeting, a deal will be struck for Peter to go to Ghana with his bodyguard (me) and be shown the dyed money. He will be shown how the dye remover works and will be lured into thinking that there are millions of dollars waiting to be 'washed' in a similar way. He will be set on a road which, if he were a real mark, would see him stripped of all of his wealth.

Of course, this all depends on us meeting the gang. There is one possible problem. I have arranged the meeting place, a hotel in central London. In normal circumstances, to keep control of the situation, they would choose the meeting place, but this time I do so I can set up the filming. I know I am taking a bit of a risk; they may feel it is a risk too far.

Peter Coles is playing the part of the lottery winner – a retired dustbin man who scooped £5.4 million – to perfection, complete with cravat and ostentatious cigars and cutter. We've invented a fictitious history for our mark. He is supposed to be married with a wife called Jackie, and pretends to have an interest in gambling. Peter has decided on using his real name in case we have to travel abroad and his passport may be seen. I do the same, though for the moment they only know me as Mac.

We wait in a hotel room which has an array of covert equipment cunningly disguised in it. There is a camera in a suitcase and a bag and I am wearing one, too. We wait some more. It's 8.30p.m. and I am getting worried that they won't show. After several calls they say they are on their way. Peter offers his advice. He doesn't think they will turn up because the location is wrong. They sense something isn't right, but they just can't put their finger on it.

Even though we have already compromised them and their operation with the footage and the tapes we've obtained, in order to kill the scam for good it has to be seen in its full glory. For that we've got to press ahead, but Peter says that I am making it too easy for them.

Apparently, the dynamic is wrong because I am the one holding all the cards, yet I'm doing all the chasing. If I was a proper villain, I would be saying, 'If you want the action, then come on. If not, then piss off.' I debate with Peter on what to say to them on the phone and the strategy we should plot from here. His experience as a policeman is obviously going to be essential for ensnaring the fraudsters. I realize I have underestimated them.

At 9.00p.m. there is still no Solomon. It's looking as if Peter is right. The debate about what to do warms up. I suggest that I phone them and give them a hard time. Peter advises me to tell them that they have put me 'in the shit' and that if they don't want a piece of the action then they shouldn't have brought us down the road this far.

I phone from the hotel room, which has more wires than your average telephone exchange.

SOLOMON:	'We're leaving now.'
DONAL:	'In all honesty, I need to have a time. I say 9.15 and if your man is not here by 9.15, my man's gone and that's the night over. So if you're not here by 9.15, it's over. I've got to construct a story to cover me now because I've gone through this whole rigmarole for you and for us…'
SOLOMON:	'We will call you.'
DONAL:	'Well, you said that ten minutes ago. The bottom line is that our man is gone at 9.15.'
SOLOMON:	'…We'll call.'

There is something wrong. Whatever it is, we have got to pull back, otherwise it is going to look too weak. We have got to think as they would think. We may be in danger ourselves if they genuinely believe that Peter is a lottery winner and decide they want to get the money in a more violent way. We discuss it and agree to pull back, for our safety and the survival of our ruse.

Five minutes later, I call Solomon. Henry, his associate, answers. I give him the run-down and end our relationship, on instructions from Peter. 'He's left the room. I'm not happy. You've put my job in danger, you have risked me, my salary and it's over. You guys haven't been here and I'm sorry about that. Thanks very much for the call but you are an hour late. Thanks very much. Take care.' The words are delivered firm and hard. We are working on the principle that, by pulling back, the fraudsters will get hungry for more action. I have been strong. Now all we can do is wait and see.

It just so happens, Peter tells me, that as we are attempting our sting on the 419 fraudsters, the seventh Annual Nigerian Crime Conference is being held in Fort Worth, Texas. It is being attended by over 500 law enforcement agents from the US, FBI, private industry, international banks and Interpol. It reminds me just how international the scam is and possibly how dangerous and difficult it is to catch the 419ers red-handed.

6th December 1998

We have contact with Solomon today. He says he was nervous about the location. The 419ers need to feel in control. They were not in control. He explains that he likes to arrange the location for safety purposes. He is going to Nigeria and Ghana over Christmas, but promises to return to complete our transaction. He says that he'll be back for business in the new year. When he comes back I will be more prepared. And I will be armed with one or two more devices to encourage Solomon to convict himself further – another ruse to sting the stingers. I will have our newspaper cutting and photographs to help move the story along and to allay any suspicions they might have of me and Peter.

8th December 1998

I slept badly last night. It was all the preparations for my return to fashion that distracted me. My work in that world involves small bursts. Journalistically, I'm a sprinter doing the 100-metre dash; on football and fraud, it's a marathon. It's difficult being a distance runner and a sprinter at the same time.

I return to Milan. I am out of practice with 'Mac' and find it hard to whip up his outrageous enthusiasm and effusive greetings of 'Ciao bello'. (It has been pointed out to me that I have been greeting every man in Milan with 'Ciao bella', the feminine form, but no one seems to have noticed other than Colin. I have pheasant Italian – it's a bit like pidgin Italian, only much worse.)

I rest and recuperate after my flight and prepare to invent the photographer's overwhelming personality again. It comes back eventually. I warm up on the phone to Metello, a PR I am keen to network with. 'Pronto, it's Mac, Metello. How are you? Well, the boy is back in town. I'm in Milano. Put on your seatbelts. I'm in town.'

In the evening I go to the city's main nightclubs, Hollywood and Shocking. I can now walk into either club with hundreds queuing outside and take anybody with me directly into the VIP sections. I am a PR's friend. It is a respect thing. Diego is inside and keen to keep me up to date on his conquests.

'I do this orgy... beautiful... Two girls. [It] One was the first time [the other model was] with a woman.'

I inquire about the points situation. He confirms that it is a twenty-pointer. He is triumphant.

'Yes, I'm winning.' And there is no concern about one of the young model's ages. 'She's seventeen.' I ponder it and repeat inquiringly, 'Seventeen?'

'She's a fucking Lolita... she has something that really excites me,' he says. '[In] The last month I have sixty-one points, I fucked like a beast.'

The standings are now even between Diego and Lino after a recent push by Diego up the rankings.

'You must be proud of yourself,' I say.

'Yeah, actually,' Diego agrees, nodding for emphasis and grinning, crow's feet scrunching round the side of his dark glasses.

At about 3.00a.m. I give up the ghost. The PA announces 'Moonsinners are in the house'. I leave.

9th December 1998

The PRs expect me to party. We arrange to meet for lunch. Nearly every one of them drops what they are doing to entertain me. Quite an honour. I begin to feel self-satisfied and self-congratulatory until I realize that these guys see me as a soft touch, as somebody they can use or leech off. It is not our great plans or strategies, but their greed that has brought me close to them and brought them to the lunch table.

There is, of course, also the little matter of my invented magazine commission. That well-known publication, *Polkadot*, for which I am also photographing a special edition on 'Milan Nightlife'. Colin, the producer, was not impressed with my chosen name, but in Milan no one seems to care. For the PRs there is either a photograph or free hospitality in it for them. They would not be here unless they thought it was in their interests.

My relationship with the PRs gives everyone else in the Milan fashion world a licence to talk with me openly. Travelling in those circles, I am perceived as an insider. I 'know the score' and they can be free with me. We meet and greet, which means a kiss on both cheeks and a hug. This is too intimate for my job, it makes the inevitable betrayal too personal. I deflect their hugs with wide elbow movements to protect my covert camera equipment from detection. At the moment it's working, so I kiss the PRs. This is Milan, and in Milan you do as the Milanese do.

Lorenzo, Oliver, Metello and Lino are there. Diego's having problems with his mobile home – or Volvo 740 as he would call it – and can't make it. I explain to the guys why I am in town outside fashion week: a bit of preparation for my supposed international exhibition, Fashion and its Fringes.

'I'm just knocking off a couple of shots. Having a bit of fun here, you know. No lighting, just lash it off.'

We shoot the breeze and now have enough material to share a few stories and laughs. Lorenzo tells me how the Arab Princes come into the clubs and buy the company of some of the top models for huge amounts of money. Football is also discussed. By now if I can hold my own with the Chelsea, I can certainly hold my own with any Italian (except Vialli) talking about English football. This is what is called in the office 'cross-fertilization'.

We all arrange to meet later. I leave the lunch with my researcher for this trip, Ben Anderson, who whispers to me, 'You had a wire sticking out at the bottom of your shirt. I was trying to kick you under the table.' It's a close shave, and not the only one. Colin, who is known to the PRs as a talent-spotter for music videos, is filming in a rented car across the road from the restaurant. Oliver kept looking over at the car during the meal and I was sure he had seen him. I was surreptitiously trying to draw my hand across my neck – sign language for 'cut'. In the event, Oliver didn't actually see Colin, or if he did, he wasn't saying so.

I am trying to use this PR friendship to get close to two men who work for Elite. One of them is a PR and about to become a live-in chaperon to models as young as thirteen. The other used to be a PR and is handing the job of chaperon over to his PR friend with the support and agreement of the agency whose girls he minds and 'protects'. For the moment, the photographer's ruse continues to open doors for me.

Diego picks me up later to go to the clubs.

'I know you think I'm an animal sometimes, but I'm trying my best,' Diego says and then looks at me. In the same conversation he tells me that 'I see myself as [a] Jeremy Irons figure in *Lolita*.' This film name is thrown up by the fashion world all the time. It is uncomfortable. I wonder how often it will be repeated to me during my sojourn in the world of fashion.

10th December 1998

After another blitz last night in the company of the PRs, I prepare to return to London. My fashion sprint is over – for the moment. Football calls.

11th December 1998

Paul's chest pains have not abated and, despite his stoic demeanour, they continue to give him concern and cause me some distress. He not only has pain, he has a growth – a lump in his chest. Today, he decides to go to the doctor.

The doctor gives him the best- and worst-case scenarios. It is either an abnormal but benign growth, or it's symptomatic of something more serious. The lump may be a consequence of a tumour on his liver. He gets an emergency appointment with a specialist for tests.

12th December 1998

Jason is not a hooligan today. Rather benignly, he is selling Christmas trees. Being a full-time hooligan is not a lucrative business, although I understand it gives a lot of job satisfaction. He still plies his tyre business but in his heart of hearts he is a full-time hooligan and part-time tree seller. Even so, Paul and I continue with our plan to drive up to Derby, where Chelsea is playing an away match at Pride Park, to maintain a presence in the football world. I am not rigged up. And, as it turns out, it's a good job too. Otherwise I would have proved more interesting to the police than would be tolerable.

I am standing outside a pub opposite Derby's main station with a number of well-known Chelsea hooligans. The police presence is huge and they are eyeing up everyone. Unfortunately, as Paul and I liaise with three other members of the production team on the mobiles, I am suddenly struck that it isn't the other hooligans who are attracting attention, it is us. Pip calls to say that he thinks we should tone down our act and Paul takes off his shades to soften the image. We still think it's funny until we realize the police are probably going to search us.

I call up another colleague, Mike, and surreptitiously give him all my credit cards and identity documents, then decide to walk to the car to see if the police interest is genuine or if I am just being paranoid. Sure enough, about ten policemen round the corner. Nice to know that when you think they are all looking at you – you're right.

They walk straight up to us and say we've been acting suspiciously, using a mobile phone too frequently. It's hardly a crime, I say to myself. For a second I put on my civil libertarian hat and then I realize they are treating me like a hooligan because I am acting the role. A search just proves we're doing a good job. Happy to congratulate myself at any opportunity, I take the body search as a compliment.

'Sir, could you take off your hat, please?' My arms are spread-eagled and held aloft while they pat me down. They ask me my details and check for any criminal convictions. I use my real name. It comes back negative. They say they are empowered to search the car and do so, but stop at breaking open the glove compartment which contains the secret camera. That would have taken some explanation. The whole process is intimidating, but may be quite useful in the long run. A number of football fans look around the corner to see who is being searched. I recognize one of them as a serious hooligan. I'm sure he won't let the incident go unnoticed. It might even get back to Jason on the grapevine.

14th December 1998

Yesterday I kept company with Jason and watched him play football. Today, I flew to Milan. He thinks I'm off to do a bit of dodgy business and will catch him later in the week. It's unlikely, but Paul should be able to spin him a few lines about where I am and when I'm coming home.

Colin is very concerned about my rehabilitation as a photographer. He tells me that he lives in mortal fear of me confusing my roles: going up to a football hooligan and advising him that, really, blue isn't his colour, or alternatively... well, you can imagine. He says that my transition is noticeable, that when I come back from working on football I'm just a little belligerent, just a little less willing to play court jester for the PRs.

16th December 1998

The ground is prepared for me to meet and photograph some of the other people on the Milan scene. Daniele and Luca are my targets. They represent the very bottom of the Elite management. Gérald Marie stands on top of this pyramid. Daniele is a PR and has been primed for my fawning attentions by the other PRs. The exhibition and the magazine served their purpose and his ego did the rest. He invites me to dinner with a number of models tonight.

The charade continues. 'What I'm really keen to do is to use you in the Milan end of the exhibition,' I explain to Daniele, buttering him up. 'My exhibition will travel with London, Milan, Paris, New York [shows] and whoever the character is from that particular city will appear in that particular exhibition.'

'Wow,' Daniele says. He is burly and baby-faced. Well, overweight actually. I heap flattery upon flattery.

'But I think you would be a great character. So what I normally do is come and get to know you, have a few beers. We'll knock off a couple of instant Polaroids tonight, but I'll grab you tomorrow for maybe an hour,' I say, arranging the next shoot in the same breath.

During the meal, Daniele explains the PR system to Ben, my researcher. When Ben summarizes it, a model at the table says it's actually very disgusting. In fact she is a girlfriend to Luca, a PR who is due to take over Daniele's job as chaperon to Elite's young models in Milan while Daniele goes off to work for Elite in New York.

Other models Lisa has talked to share this assessment. They feel used and exploited but sometimes think that they are having a good time. Daniele says things have changed. These days the girls are younger and he goes into nightclubs where the models are fourteen, fifteen and sixteen. He misses the old days. 'Women, tits and ass. That's what I like.' It seems to be a shared view among the PRs. Although they say this, it doesn't seem to have changed the PR system or the way they treat the models. Fifteen- or sixteen-year old models have become the norm.

17th December 1998

It's about 10.30a.m. and I'm on my way by taxi to the offices of Elite in Milan. Daniele is there and getting ready to be photographed by me. My colleague, Ben, who is playing a role as a friend and camera assistant, and I are both wearing tee-shirt cameras, in case one breaks down. I walk ahead of him so he can film me entering the impressive-looking building. To the side of the Elite office is a residency where the youngest Elite models from thirteen to eighteen stay while they are in Milan. Daniele's job for the last ten years has been to look after these girls. During that time he has been an active and paid PR for the nightclubs, a conflict of interest that doesn't seem to attract too much attention here.

He takes me and my researcher to the lounge in the residency and, under the guise of a photoshoot, talks to me. He is surrounded by huge, poster-size magazine covers of some of the models he has met over the years. Many of them stayed at the residence. His physique is that of an ex-bodybuilder gone to pot: fat, but broad-shouldered. Upon reflection he looks a bit like me. I get him to introduce himself to the lens, ostensibly to relax him but primarily to allow the viewer at home to watch him.

'My name is Daniele. I'm thirty one. I'm a PR.' I am trying to build up an evidential case against Daniele and challenge him about working as a PR and a chaperon for Elite at the same time. He is slightly nervous about having his photo taken, but I don't think he is suspicious of my gentle interrogation between shots.

'I have no idea how you survived working for Elite during the day and then working as a PR at night. I have no idea, I mean you must have been...?'

'Well, I did. I don't know how, but I did. Everybody think I was crazy, but now I think about it I think, wow, I don't know how I did. I mean, you look back and think you are crazy, why you do this stuff.'

The dual roles are perfectly compatible, not on moral grounds but on practical ones, although it means getting very little sleep. He was working at the office during the day, helping to sort out the schedules for the girls, chaperoning them at night and, if he could, taking them to the nightclubs where he would get paid for their presence. Whereas other PRs had to go to other residencies and pick models up from various castings, Daniele had a ready-made supply of models. He lived with them. He 'looked after' them. Some of them were as young as thirteen. Even he recognizes the problem with young models in Milan. 'Too young girls, too inexperienced for this job, they come here, they get laid and get fucked.'

I ask him if I can photograph his tattoos. I know all about them. The other PRs have told me about them in detail. I see a massive tattoo of an eagle on his back, which he says took twelve hours to do. My little one for football took thirty minutes and was one of the most painful experiences I've ever had. He leans against the wall, head bowed, and continues to talk. He looks vulnerable now. There is talk about sex and drugs. In this world they go hand in hand.

He explains that in the last ten years working at Elite he has met over 12,000 models and taken about 2,000 to the clubs. 'I don't know why I have this energy, why they talk to me and not somebody else.' He says that his models trust him and confide in him. And not only that. He tells me he's slept with over 325 models. He's collected the model cards, detailing the girls' vital statistics, that the agencies produce, one for each model he has been to bed with. Despite the age of some of the girls in his residency, he thinks nothing of walking around in his underwear and reluctantly admits to having relationships with some of the girls. 'It's like, if you like someone, she like you and you live in the same place, it is very easy to connect the two thing[s] together.' The minute he mentions this he gets nervous and wants to wind up the session. I try to distract him.

He is reluctant to explore this indiscretion for obvious reasons. He is trying to move on. He is trying to leave his wild times with sex and drugs behind him as he moves up the Elite corporate ladder. And they were extreme.

'For me they was wild, I don't know, you sleep with two girls with your friends. Me and Oliver have two room-mates so we fuck all them in the same room, or going around drunk, we go round naked with the girls, all around the residency... we take speed and you go to the park at five o'clock in the morning with twenty girls and everybody fucked up.'

Daniele says the agency is his home. They are his family. He says he cares for the models as if they were his sisters. Some brother.

Later, I speak to Luca, Daniele's super sub or replacement at the Elite chaperon for young models. He was a PR until recently when he took over Daniele's job. Luca is muscular, fit and in his early twenties. He has a pregnant girlfriend (the one critical of PRs last night), and is strangely disturbed by my line of questioning – to the extent that he says he recognizes the malevolent risks attached to sending young models to Milan. 'I think that it is not so good for a young girl to come to Milan. It is not,' he says.

'Why's that?' I inquire.

'Because I think for a girl like fifteen or sixteen or so it's very dangerous being in Milano, with the parties, you know, but anyway, all the people around them go like that [he cups his hands and closes in, making a crushing motion] – the vulture,' he says expressing his concern.

'The vultures. Well, that is interesting, if they're fourteen, fifteen, sixteen – that whole age group, then they must be quite vulnerable because it's their first time in a big city,' I say, trying to explore his openness a fraction further.

'And the point, the girls that are eighteen, nineteen, twenty, they really good, you know. The problem are the really, really young girls, because... in America, they can't drink, they can't go out to a club, they can do nothing in the States. They arrive here, they can drink what they want, they can go out when they want, they can go to club and nobody will say nothing. So it's like Disneyland for them, know what I mean?'

Luca looks at me intensely. He is emphatic. He knows he's got an impossible job. He's got to try and protect the girls from his own friends. The same friends who are doing the same PR job that he was doing just a month ago. As Luca says himself: he's not going to turn his friends away.

I fly back to London, Stansted, arriving at 11.00p.m. It's still a long way to my bed. First, I return to the BBC offices to collect some tapes for tomorrow's new assignment, then I go home and get my 'care assistant' kit together before driving through the night to get to a hotel close to the care home, which is to be my temporary base. Lee's short tenure at the home has confirmed that there is cause for concern. Yesterday, he filmed the Christmas concert, which was a very sad and moving occasion. He has witnessed bullying and shouting and what he thinks is poor practice. I hope I can handle this fittingly. Tomorrow I will join him at the home. It's my first day there and his last.

18th December 1998

I get lost on the way to the home and stuck in traffic and am late for work. They aren't pleased and I say I will try to do better.

The care industry is an issue I've wanted to explore for some time. It's light years away from my investigations into football, fashion and fraud, and I welcome the chance to draw in my horns from those high-pressure 'lifestyles' and focus on something more observational and introverted. My character reflects that, too. 'Mike' is quiet and easy-going and calm – the antithesis of Mac the photographer and Macca. In fact, I'm so low-key that the staff make a point of commenting on it – 'Oh, we need someone calm like you around here.' It's a relief to tone things down, but I don't do it deliberately. Something about being in the home does it for me. As an untrained care assistant I want to do my job as any other assistant would do and, other than that, be a neutral force within the home. Some of the patients warm to me immediately, and such open warmth is unusual in any of my other fields or in society generally. Remember, any one of us could be here. The clients are all here by slender twists of fate.

That is my mantra. We are all equal in terms of humanity, though not in terms of responsibility – that is the mantra at the home. I am here to find out if indeed we are all equal on those terms.

There are also questions about myself. I've come to see if I have the patience and fortitude to be a good and caring worker. That way, I can explore the pressures care workers are faced with and discover whether those pressures are expressed in untoward behaviour.

There is no training today because they can't find the manuals. I join in with the rest of the care workers, but I am a novice and I just shadow the other workers on the job.

19th December 1998

Back to being a hooligan for a few hours. I find it easier to switch from care worker to hooligan because my own personality is closer to that of the care role than, I hope, that of the hooligan. I return to London for the Chelsea vs Tottenham game. The match is uneventful. Chelsea win 2–0. Still, I am there to be seen and it works – some of the old faithful in the Fulham Dray acknowledge me.

After the game, I prepare to drive to the hotel, which is about an hour from the care home. I am due there at seven in the morning for a fourteen-hour shift.

20th December 1998

It's a privilege to work with some of the adults with learning difficulties here. It is a pleasure to strike up bonds with some of these patients, or clients, as they are called here. It's hard to pinpoint what it is that's so uplifting about working with them – and how disturbing it is then, to hear one worker whisper in the ear of one patient, 'Shut the fuck up'. The client has an IQ of a four-year-old.

Today I learn about control and restraint procedures, which they use when clients are being difficult. These are now officially called 'care and responsibility' procedures. Unofficially, care workers use the term 'decking'. Not a medically recognized term, I suspect. From what I can see, it means putting a 'difficult' patient on the floor and holding his wrists back until he stops being difficult or until drugs can be administered to calm him down. It might also mean just sitting on a patient until he/she calms down, as recounted to me by one member of staff.

22nd December 1998

My covert equipment for the care work has been tailored to allow me to wear normal clothes like lumberjack shirts and jeans. As I am indoors most of the time it would be unusual to wear too many layers so I have to spread the equipment around my body. Essentially, it means sending some of the equipment down my legs and dispersing the rest on only one side of my body. It takes an hour's preparation before I go into the field. I have a mini-disc running for sound nearly all the time and carry three video tapes a day with me. I try to record all my interactions so that, if someone makes a complaint once I've left the field, in all likelihood I will have the evidence. I am told today that I can expect a fire drill at some stage. Later, I learn that one member of staff let off a fire extinguisher at a patient to try and control him. I don't expect that to be part of my fire training.

23rd December 1998

Another eight hours at the home. It is tough, personally and journalistically. It is tiring and of course I am tired from my other work and could do with a break. But I can't afford to take one. Not being an expert, I can't be sure if someone is doing anything wrong, unless, of course, it is an admission or it is overwhelmingly obvious. It's Christmas week and I haven't bought anybody presents. Christmas is off for me this year.

24th December 1998

Christmas Eve and I am working in the care home. I finished at nine today. With the drive to the hotel and 'de-riggings' it's nearly a quarter to midnight before I have any time to myself.

It's been a traumatic day too. A care worker just left me with the thought that, not only is pain accidentally inflicted on some of the patients in the home, but certainly, in his words, it is necessary and is probably a good thing because he would want to use it as a means of control.

The worker tells me that 'I've seen some people hit some of the clients, you know, when they've been [hit first] in the face and if there is no one around, they might do it back. I personally don't, but there you go. I'm not saying it's wrong, I just don't do it.'

The accepted official line is that the 'care and responsibility' (control and restraint) procedures don't cause pain. But that view is not necessarily shared by the staff.

'I know it's awful again but unless they are suffering a certain amount of pain, they are going to carry on what they're doing. Of course that's not what the bosses want to hear,' says one.

I feel tender because I would normally be at home with family and friends preparing for a special day. Feeling tender, too, because a story is told to me that I feel little satisfaction in recording. Another worker also outlines a story to me about a client. Describing the client as 'horrible', she tells how he was being troublesome and so was held down and rolled up in a carpet for twenty minutes, so he couldn't move and cause any more difficulties.

'We rolled him up in a carpet, once had a big carpet downstairs. We rolled him up in a carpet 'cos he was, oh, a long time ago, so bad we couldn't do anything with him. So we just rolled him up in a carpet. Just left him to it... Better than sitting on him and holding him down and he wasn't getting hurt...'cos he marks ever so easily, doesn't he? He bruises very easy and he gets carpet burn ever so easy so we just rolled him up in a carpet and just sat back and watched him basically.'

You wouldn't do that to a dog, I thought, but you would happily joke about inflicting this upon a young man with learning difficulties.

25th December 1998

It is a genuine treat to see the adults with learning difficulties who are variously challenged in many ways enjoy their Christmas. They open their presents with wide-eyed excitement, thrilled at the prospect of a visit from Santa later. The chairman of the company that runs the home dresses up and distributes presents to the clients. I am a sentimental Christmas fan.

My own Christmases are usually replete with tradition, right down to the Christmas-morning swim. This year there is no swim. There is no family fun and drinks with neighbours. But there is the memorable warmth of a tender and loving Christmas greeting from some of the clients. In many ways, the care worker represents the extended family for those who have no family around them today.

Today, the clients are my extended family, as I am theirs.

In spite of this special day, a care worker – wearing a party hat – liberates himself of his frustration by waving a fist in front of a patient, saying, 'You can have this as well'. The same worker illuminates me with some of his other techniques. We are sitting down with some clients and his open conversation is liberally interrupted by some of them. He isn't speaking confidentially but matter-of-factly. That is the surprise. It is no secret. It is normal banter.

'Someone who is actually really good actually is X because you can actually punch him... like you can muck about with him and go up to him and... and smack. So as long as you're careful and you know what you are doing and you ain't going to hurt him too much... 'cos his brothers used to do boxing with him as well.'

'So he is quite happy to be punched?' I inquire.

'Yeah, 'cos he thinks it's a big game. So I mean that is quite handy sometimes, 'cos you can get frustrated at X [and], bang [simulating punch], and it's out – you just get on with your work.' He estimates that if he told an average person on the street this story they wouldn't be too happy with it. I paraphrase public opinion.

'You shouldn't be punching somebody to get out your frustration?'

'But in a way it's good for him and it's a way of getting it our [out] for you, isn't it?' the worker explains.

I start work at 7.00a.m. and finish at 9.00p.m. I get to the hotel and take off the equipment. There are people spending Christmas at the hotel. I wanted to work today at the home but, in all honesty, I didn't want to return here. I go to my room, my Christmas over.

27th December 1998

The river calls me today. I go for a paddle. My very own Christmas present to me. Despite stealing some time for myself, my mind is still on the care home. Today I have to remind myself to ensure that the bank accounts are in place to handle my wages, moving the cheques from a dormant account in the name of Mike Mac Intyre to a newly opened BBC bank account. It is important that the money the care home pays me remains untouched, so it can be returned after I have finished the investigation. There are so many small but essential details that need to be carefully considered in this case to ensure I'm not in breach of the law or behaving unethically. For all that, the river occupies most of my thoughts.

29th December 1998

Today, the head of the care home was concerned about my being taken on. Apparently she gave me a job without checking references or doing a police check. I shouldn't be allowed to work with vulnerable groups unless I've been fully vetted. I tell them I'll get them references. I've already given them addresses, which they haven't followed up. Now they want phone numbers for my referees – urgently.

1st January 1999

Out of the field and in Ireland, my New Year resolutions are to give up caffeine and nail-biting. I wish I could give up some easier addiction such as alcohol or drugs. I have no will power – none whatsoever. Before I know it, I have drunk a mug of coffee and nibbled the cuticle on the little finger of my left hand. I resolve immediately to give up all resolutions.

3rd January 1999

After a brief trip across the water to see in the New Year, I return to the home to find more panic. One of the clients has been bruised on his face after being restrained. The senior carer on duty refused to counter-sign the explanation given for the use of the procedure. Various members of staff blame each other. I see the patient. He has redness on his forehead and a mark on his nose. I am assured that he looked a lot worse yesterday.

I work another fourteen-hour shift. It is hard work, make no mistake. There is a bus ride today for the clients. We leave the home at about 4.30p.m. in the bus. We return at 8.00p.m. No one has been allowed out of the bus for three-and-a-half hours except a client who went to the toilet, and me. We are given a McDonald's at around 5.30p.m. and we drive around – to view the sights, I suppose, though it is dark by five. In my inexpert view, many of the clients are distressed and bored by this strange trip. Any purpose to it is unclear to me.

7th January 1999

My last day in the home for a while. I intend to phone them later in the week to say that I've had a personal crisis in Ireland and have to go back there. I will return, hopefully, but I am going to leave to assess the evidence. I may have to come back to verify certain practices before we take our investigation to the relevant authorities. It's a late finish.

Before I end my tenure there, I see an incontinent patient being shooed down the corridor with a broom because he has soiled himself. This is distressing. These scenes seem to be a regular feature of life at the home. It has been a disturbing, yet personally rewarding Christmas. All the same, it is one that I never wish to repeat.

9th January 1999

Haematology is not a word that was familiar to me. It is now. Moreover, it has become all too familiar to Paul. He has his blood tests today, preliminary signposts to cancer or not as the case may be, and as we all hope. He has not had time off work other than to go to the hospital or the doctor. All the while he is still playing my hooligan partner. And playing it superbly, despite this burden, this very personal weight on his shoulders.

Word has come from news agencies that one of the kingpins of the Nigerian 419 fraud, a Chief Victor Okafor has been killed in a car accident over the holiday period. I wonder if he is Solomon's boss. He was regarded as one of the architects of the scam and had apparently earned millions from it. I presume that his death will mean that there is a battle in Nigeria to, replace him at the top of the lucrative 419 hierarchy. This may delay Solomon's return from Nigeria.

12th January 1999

There was no sleep to be had last night. It had nothing to do with the double espresso I had before I went to bed. It had everything to do with the fact that I have to make a very nervous call to Gérald Marie to try and follow up on Milan last year. How do I interest a man who plays in the company of supermodels and earns millions a year? Am I just going to ring up on the off-chance that he might invite me out for dinner again? I have no confidence that I have anything to offer this man to encourage him to get to know me better.

13th January 1999

Today I make the call to Gérald Marie. I say that I will be in Paris for just a few days and will bring him up to speed on my adventures when I see him. I hint at whorehouses and excess. He is welcoming. I am relieved.

15th January 1999

Fly out to Paris. I get to the hotel and start calling Gérald's mobile. I get the him on the phone and say that I've just dropped in en route to the US, where I am photographing Chelsea Clinton, but I am in Paris for a few days and I ask him if we can meet up. He seems pleased to hear from me and gives me his secretary's number to arrange a lunch appointment. I call ten minutes too late and his lunch diary is full. The secretary encourages me to phone after three and she says that she'll try and fit me in. I call at three and there is no joy. Gérald is not back from lunch. I call at four and he is still not back. I feel like I am pushing too hard. I ring again. Finally he answers his mobile and we arrange to meet at the Bain Douche nightclub for 1.00a.m.

16th January 1999

Three o'clock in the morning at Le Bain Douche. No Gérald. I return to the hotel and collect Colin, the producer, and we go for an early-morning coffee. We decide it's time to pull back and pack our bags. We are back in London for 9.30a.m. I get a taxi from Waterloo, go home and change my wardrobe. Off goes the fashion photographer's get-up and on goes the shades, the baseball hat, the Tommy Hilfiger jacket, the loathsome Ralph Lauren light-blue jeans and the absolutely detested white classic Reebok trainers.

It's Chelsea vs Coventry at the Bridge. It ends in victory for Chelsea (2–1). The score doesn't interest me. There is nothing to report except that Jason is again eating fried chicken after the game. He is – as he would say – 'cushty' with me. He doesn't yet know if he is going to Oxford next week. Chelsea are playing Oxford in the FA Cup and with all the passions that that entails it could be a potential flashpoint. Oxford has a large hooligan firm and trouble is expected.

In the evening I phone Gérald's mobile. His answering service is on and I leave a message to say how sorry I am that I couldn't make it to the Bain Douche last night. I got detained. 'See you in Milan. Ciao, Mac.' I am being strong. I don't want him to think I'm running pathetically after him – which, of course, I am.

17th January 1999

A team meeting at the BBC's offices in White City. I thank them all for their extraordinary commitment. They are great and whenever I am flagging they pick me up and whenever I get uppity they are quick enough to put me in my place.

18th January 1999

News of a death threat against me comes today from the offices of *World In Action*. 'Tell him that if he testifies he's a dead man.' I phone Scotland Yard and the investigating team and we weigh it up. No great need to be stressed out, we agree. The threat is low-grade but, if I'm worried, they say that they will investigate further. The threat emanates from the bogus weddings investigation I conducted for *World in Action*. There is a court case (R vs Moonesinghe and others) in March, but it doesn't concern me too much. I forget about it. Frankly, I'm more worried about Paul, who is awaiting further tests to discover if he has a tumour on his liver. Now that is a death threat.

19th January 1999

We have a very distressed Jason on our hands. The police raided an address where they thought he was staying and turned it upside-down for drugs. He adds things up very mechanically in his mind as he clunks logically from one proposition to another.

'The thing is, mate, that they got the wrong fucking place,' Jason says. He says he'll 'kill the fucker who grassed him up'. Fortunately, it is obvious that no one who knows him would give the wrong address, so we are exonerated. Not only that, but the fact that he feels secure enough to confide in us means we've moved a notch higher on his totem pole.

25th January 1999

It's Oxford vs Chelsea in the FA Cup tonight. We – Paul, Mike, Lee and I – arrive by train and are manhandled and pushed and shoved by the police – and rightly so. The company we are keeping is on the verge of rioting at any time, but tight policing ensures there are only minor skirmishes.

The game ends in a 1–1 draw. Dramatically Vialli scores the equalizer five minutes from the end. The final whistle blows and the Oxford fans, denied the victory that seemed in the bag, race onto the pitch and try to break through police lines to attack us. Seeing this, the Chelsea fans try to scale the fence onto the pitch to respond. The police keep both sides in check, herding the Chelsea fans onto buses to be taken back to the station, out of harm's way. The singing and chanting on the bus is offensive; the worst I've ever heard. But this *is* Chelsea. They launch into their anti-Semitic fireside favourites: 'I've got a foreskin, haven't you/I've got a foreskin, haven't you…' to the tune of 'She'll be Coming Round the Mountain'. Another is led by some bard at the back of the bus.

'I went to a party one Saturday night,
I went, some Tottenham wanted a fight,
So I pulled out my razor, as quick as a flash,
And said Chelsea rule London, fucking Yid trash.'

Lee has a secret camera recording the festivities. He stands up to get the pictures on the bus. I realize he looks too obvious and worry he might get spotted. There are a lot of unsavoury characters here: no main men that I recognize but a lot of troops seem to be up for a fight. I catch his eye and run my finger along my neck, mouthing 'cut'. He does. It is depressing having to record this behaviour. I will be glad when this is over.

At the station, the police dogs have been brought out. We are packed onto the train. On the way back to Reading, where we have parked the car, I hear a young Reading supporter chat about violence. This could be interesting, I think, so I introduce myself and Lee. Nothing more is said, though, and we part company at Reading. (Chelsea and Reading are sister firms. They often travel and fight together. Andy 'Nightmare' Frain is also a leader of the Reading firm and is up in court in March for attacking a mounted police officer at an Oxford–Reading game last season. Footballing enmities and hatreds are shared and they travel together. Alliances are forged and continue long after the reasons that united them have been forgotten.)

It's my birthday. I call my twin. I go to bed. Another year older... I feel like I'm twice our ages – I feel sixty-six.

Sleep doesn't come easy at the moment. Worry. I have been thinking about an invite from Jason which has been loosely extended to us to attend a protest march in the company of Combat 18 and other Head-hunters this Saturday. I'll think and sleep some more.

27th January 1999

Paul has a big day today. He has been told that he may have liver cancer and is going in for crucial tests this morning. I phone him before he goes in and I know that he is just being brave. He is my right-hand man in football and *is* brave, I know that, but today he is putting it on. He is scared. I am scared. He has looked very tired recently and has not been well. Last week he vomited three times in one day. It is looking very serious. The whole team is terrified for him but keen not to display it. He says he just wants to get through this and get the work done. All the while he has had this over his head he has tried to keep busy, working every hour God sends. He is due out of hospital this evening.

I phone him later. The blood tests are done. There is some trace of the cancer, but it's benign. He is emotional. He is clear. Thank God.

29th January 1999

Still not sleeping well.

30th January 1999

Every Christmas Day my friends and I go for a swim in the River Liffey. It is cold. Always very cold. As we sup hot ports and wolf down mince pies afterwards, we are all unanimous in our opinion that (as usual) it was the coldest swim ever.

I am reminded of that day. Today I keep saying to myself, 'This is the most dangerous ever'. I think that today I am right.

For days I have been trying to downplay my Southern Irish accent and reinvent myself as a Northern Irish extreme Loyalist, as we plan to join the right-wing terrorist group Combat 18 and the National Front in an attack on an Irish Republican march in central London. It commemorates the fourteen Catholics killed on Bloody Sunday in 1972. My accent might very well betray me to other extremists from Northern Ireland but probably not to any of the Chelsea brethren.

My *Accents for Actors* tape went with me everywhere this week but it was a disaster. I have never done any acting or had any training with accents. I am only just competent at delivering my own accent and completely useless at anyone else's. I retreat to my very own pronunciation of the ubiquitous phrase 'deead ooonnn', harsh at the beginning and soft at the end.

As I decamp at Waterloo in the company of four other BBC colleagues (Paul, 'Snapper', Lee and Mike), I am greeted with a familiar scene of haircuts, scowls and scars. I have seen these faces before but Combat 18 and the National Front is new territory. This is a gathering of minds, thugs, politics and angry men, some of whom know why they are angry and some whom are just angry.

The atmosphere is tense. We are weighed up and do our own assessing. It is a day for eye contact and a day to be strong. Everybody gathers at Burger King on the concourse. I observe others in our disaffected clan, all of whom are here on some semblance of patronage – all, I am sure, with more history in the group than us.

I choose to wear my body-rig camera. This has to be filmed, it's my job. No one else is wearing secret equipment – it's too dangerous. There are concerns over exposure by police, thugs and Head-hunters. I wear the kit because it's my responsibility to record these events. I turn it on in Waterloo, while the police trawl through us and pace up and down with their own video cameras, saving the pictures for Intelligence. There are firms from Chelsea, Manchester, Peterborough and Belfast – and, though the police don't know it – the BBC.

Messages start to circulate. Jason and Andy Frain are organizing a new meet away from the police at a pub in Charing Cross. However, the police are one jump ahead of us. By the time we get there, they have closed the pub and are busy searching groups of fans. Time to de-rig, I realize.

I call up one of our team and grab a toilet cubicle in Charing Cross station, changing from a cameraman to a badly dressed thug. Luckily, five minutes later I am stopped and searched under section 40 of the Police and Criminal Evidence Act. Name and address and date of birth: that is the law and that is what I adhere to. Anything beyond that (or an admission of my true undercover role) could put me and others in danger, notwithstanding the fact that there were groups of our clan looking on. They are proud of me and salute Paul and me as we are searched. I acknowledge the respect. To them I am standing my ground; I am one of them. The police certainly think so.

'Distinguishing features?' one asks politely. Another takes my photograph for the files.

'I have this scar on my nose,' I say.

'Where did you get that then?' he inquires. I tell him I got it in violent circumstances when I was four and a half. We discuss an old surfing injury on my chin and my politics. 'Other distinguishing marks?' I am asked. In the mayhem, I fail by accident to mention that most recent of distinguishing features, my tattoo. (I know subconsciously that it doesn't distinguish me one little bit.) When they are satisfied, finally, I am released to find my adopted brethren.

The attack is launched from a pub on Panton Street. One hundred-strong of Head-hunters, Combat 18, National Front and five BBC journalists. I am still recording sound – I put my mini-disc on again after the first search.

Jason is loving it. He is drinking Ballygowan Irish mineral water, an unlikely drink for Jason I think and I tell him so. 'What's this Fenian water, mate?'

'I don't give a fuck. That's ammunition, mate. A bottle is a bottle to me. I don't give a fuck as long as it hits one of those cunts,' he says, putting me right.

Jason, too, was searched along with his mate. 'The geezer that I got pulled with as well... He's fucking...he's off his head.' He says that the police asked his friend if he had any convictions and his mate said that he had none. There was a crackle over the police radio and a policeman came back to him and said: 'You've murdered, you've done time for murder.' Jason picks up the story and repeats what his friend then says to the police, "You can't bring up my past." Jason laughs.

In the pub, too, is the same guy who Lee and I met coming home from the Oxford vs Chelsea game. His name is Danny. He has long, unkempt hair and a trademark blue coat and overhanging hood to protect him from CCTV. I feel sure that we (the team) are going to get to know him a little bit better if we survive this mêlée.

The attack is clearly imminent. I am chain-smoking and trying to look involved. I have a problem. Obviously another police search is a huge possibility and my microphone poses a major dilemma. I walk over to the men's toilet and try to enter a cubicle. It is occupied. Someone is doing 'Charlie' (cocaine). When he stops snorting and relinquishes the space, I flush the microphone down the loo. I am delighted to see it go down first flush. (The mini-disc recorder is a legitimate possession in the eyes of the police and hooligans – it's the microphone that distinguishes it from the music player.) Soon after that, a call is received from a Combat 18 spotter. 'We are on.' An unlikely army, we march purposefully to the back of the National Gallery, intent on action. Nightmare runs past me, shouting, 'I want to be at the front where I belong!' He is coked out of his head.

The walk breaks into a mad dash across Trafalgar Square, but the Republican marchers do not yet see us. Bottles and sticks are thrown and the head of our mob nearly breaks into the head of the Bloody Sunday Commemoration march. I am towards the rear playing catch-up, desperately trying to appear to be involved but determined not to be involved. My senses are in hyper-drive. Blood rushes to my head. I feel the redness in my eyes. I look around to see if the team is safe. Snapper is too far ahead of me. I pull him back. Tourists and pigeons are fleeing. There is huge momentum to the attack. All around, people are reacting to a burgeoning riot in central London. Sirens and flashing blue lights start up. I see the police mobilize and in one sweep they gather about sixty of us up against a wall, hemming us in as the marchers file past.

I am on the front line. Thugs, Head-hunters, Combat 18, the National Front – and the BBC – we are all there: shoulder to shoulder, man to man, we are together – we are one. Chanting with the Nazi salute: 'No surrender! No surrender! No surrender to the IRA Scum!' to the tune of 'Sing Hosannah'.

I reflect that we have protected our cover from everyone today, including the police and Special Branch, who took a particular interest in the new faces. I wonder if it is going to mean a night in the cells. I feel secure in the knowledge that I didn't commit any offence, but the 'catch-all' police operation may not be too sympathetic to this line, not least because I cannot tell them I am a journalist (though to some policemen, this is an offence in itself).

As the St George chant goes up to full revs, someone next to me who I've never met before is shouting like it is more important than life itself. I catch a slow-motion glimpse and in the intensity of the moment the spittle from his spiteful, strained face seems suspended in mid air. My senses, attuned perfectly to the situation, make out Jason's voice in the tumult. He nods in my direction. I can see he is proud of his boys and wants everyone to know that we are his men. Welcome to the brotherhood. We have come a long way since Marseilles.

The Combat 18 flag is pulled over my head and in that split second when I can't see anything and no one can see me, I retreat to a softer place, an old country house in Co. Cavan near the border on the southern side. I remember the first time I saw a television at close quarters. My twin and I hugged armchairs in the big house and I remember watching this box in the corner with shapes on it that moved. I knew there was some sort of trouble. People in the room were upset, but we were allowed to stay up late to watch for the first time. We were excited but trying not to be, in case someone really noticed us and sent us to bed. The day was Bloody Sunday.

Then the flag is gone and a tall, middle-aged woman with a red face and bulging eyes catches my eye and shouts, 'You fucking Nazi scum'. She is giving the V-sign with both hands to me, safe in the knowledge that she is on the right side of the police lines, as well as being on the side of right.

Nightmare faces up to her on the edge of the scuffle. His face is contorted and every expletive is animated by his bigoted conviction that it is he who is on the right side.

'See this', he says with a nasal twang after his cocaine binge. He points to his forehead. 'I'll smash your fucking head with it.' Jutting forward and back like a badly sprung rocking chair, Nightmare is coughing up venom. He is the most hateful person I have ever met. He knows no limits. Prison and police hold no terrors for him; he just doesn't care.

Jason – 'The Penguin' – has another flag, a repugnant (to him) Irish tricolour. He brings his lighter to it and struggles and struggles to set it afire, thumb and index finger flicking furiously. His skin is scuffed and singed by the useless flame and eventually he gives up and resorts to stamping his mark on the flag on the ground. 'Fucking Fenian bastards! Fucking Fenian bastards!' he roars.

The head of Combat 18 is standing beside me. We are the same height. Our profiles are both running with the sweat of our angry mob. He chants to the tune of 'She'll Be Coming Round the Mountain When She Comes' and I join in:

> Do you want a can of coke, Bobby Sands?
> Do you want a can of coke, Bobby Sands?
> Do you want a can of coke?
> I hope you fucking choke,
> Do you want a can of coke, Bobby Sands?

Bobby Sands was an IRA prisoner who died while on hunger strike. The thought occurs to me, as I stand among my new friends, that whatever venom they had reserved for the marchers, I represent all their enemies in one. I am Southern Irish, from a Catholic family, and a BBC journalist. Out of anyone in London that day, I have the least right to be standing where I am standing. Fleetingly, I ask myself what I am doing here. I look at Paul over this madding crowd. He looks at Snapper and we share unspoken thoughts together. 'It'll be all right,' Paul seems to be saying. I am looking after Snapper and whisper in his ear to just abide by the law and not to divulge anything to the police outside his legal requirement. I am terrified to think what will happen if we get arrested. However innocent we are, it will take a lot of explaining to the police, lawyers and the BBC Board of Governors.

In this stand-off, Jason puts in a request. He's looking for a fag. He turns towards us and asks, 'Paul, got a fag, mate?' It is another anointment of sorts – except Jason doesn't smoke.

A policeman beside me shivers with adrenaline. He is scared but dealing with it by playing games with us, staring and scowling at my fellow protestors. It is strangely intimate. He is pushed up close to me and seems to be breathing my oxygen. We are nearly cheek to cheek. He must think I am scum. I think he is doing a good job.

After the march has passed, one by one we are singled out for more searches. Strange times. Six years ago, I reported on this annual march for the *Sunday Tribune* newspaper in Ireland. Then, too, it was attacked by the far Right. I saw the thugs being searched. Today, I am a thug. I wonder who's reporting for the *Sunday Tribune* today and what they'll be doing in six years' time.

'Where were you born? Which side of the border and where was your father born?' the policeman asks. I reply, equivocally, on the right side of the border in case I incriminate myself in this company. Two police photographers are on hand to catch both profiles (my good side and bad).

I have grown up since I began this investigation. No longer is a search an imploding psychological experience. This is my sixth search in as many months. A television cameraman captures this apparent humiliation and tries to film me as I walk off after the police let me go. I do what any decent hooligan would do – hide my face and put my hand up to the camera. No insult intended, particularly as the cameraman is working for us.

After the search Paul and I disperse from the other hooligans, move away from Leicester Square and join up with Snapper, Mike and Lee. I shake their hands. Today, they endured extraordinary stress and emerged unscathed and safe. I am proud of the team – all of whom ran the gauntlet of Combat 18 and the National Front for the BBC. The rest of the supporting cast, organized by Pip, filming the events as they unfolded were not immune from danger and performed bravely and efficiently.

A day's work done. We drift out of central London for a few beers and pizza. At the end the others all go home to tell their families nothing of what happened and I return home on my own. That's the kind of business we are in.

1st February 1999

I have been sacked from the care home. Not for any impropriety but because I could not do my full-time job. There is no rancour from my end and they are quite conciliatory, too. They explain that my 'current period of unauthorized absence is unacceptable' and they have to terminate my employment as a consequence. The head of the home says that I can come down to talk about further work when I have sorted out my personal situation. They seem keen to have me back. I am keen to return.

2nd February 1999

It's frosty, but bright – a good day to wear my beloved shades – and I enter the office in breezy mood. And then it is blown away. There's been another death threat. I feel physically winded. My first response is fury. The threat came in on Friday and today is Tuesday – why wasn't I told earlier? A BBC Investigator, who has been summoned, explains there was some confusion over the name – it was reported as a threat to Daniel MacIntyre. I am petulant until I realize he did try to contact me as soon as he knew, and I apologize for my outburst. Stress is getting the better of me. The vein on the side of my forehead starts to pump and pump. What road have I gone down, I ask myself.

The threat relates, once again, to the investigation I did for *World In Action* on bogus weddings, which is the subject of court action shortly. There have been numerous arrests and one extradition from Canada, but we still have no leads on where the threats – this is my second – could have come from. What's becoming clearer is that for me, this kind of threat is likely to become a familiar fixture in my life, especially after the series has been transmitted.

I put my shades – my blinkers – back on. They are my favourites, a pair of surfing Oakleys, out of fashion now but at least they are rose-tinted.

4th February 1999

My tattoo is troubling me. There are times when I get this awful deadening resistance, like a tightening in my arm. It's not in the muscle; the sensation is subcutaneous. I've been getting it maybe once a week since I got my skin etched. Psychosomatic, I am sure, but nonetheless it feels very real to me. A friend of mine said, 'It's not that you don't like your arm, it's that your arm doesn't like you.'

Best not to go down that road, else we will hear the sound of white coats flapping.

6th February 1999

To the tune of Rod Stewart's 'Sailing':

> We are Millwall,
> We are Millwall,
> No one likes us,
> We don't care.
> Super Millwall,
> Super Millwall...

Our charge of the (far) right brigade last Saturday has earned us a special invitation to violence: an away day with the Millwall firm. It comes from Danny, or 'Super Dan' as the BBC team call him. Danny is a part of the Reading–Chelsea axis, led by Nightmare/ Andy Frain, and is a friend to one of the main Millwall men. Danny doesn't support Millwall, but is up for a fight. We travel up to Manchester with Danny and his friends on the train, having 'accidentally' bumped into them on the concourse at Euston.

Danny shoots the breeze and the more he seeks to ingratiate himself with me, the more he inadvertently incriminates himself. I am making much more progress with Danny, and more speedily, than with any other hooligan.

There are a number of reasons for this. The first and most important is patronage. I am a friend of Jason's (The Penguin) and The Penguin is a friend of Nightmare's (Andy Frain), therefore I am safe.

I am, as the street would have it, a 'proper' person. Danny is clearly more impressionable than the Old Guard, and therefore more vulnerable. More than that, he is seduced by my ostentatious trappings of wealth: the Mercedes, the designer gear and the occasional wads of cash I let him catch a glimpse of. It is at moments like this that you realize that the months of drinking in Hampton, all the clues and all our choreography and planning is paying major dividends.

Danny has a flat pug's face and a smile which stretches like the Joker's from *Batman*. He is banned from every football ground in the country – indeed, any sporting event in Europe – and is facing court for GBH and violent disorder, having hit someone around the head with an oar.

'I'll do at least six months, I reckon.'

Although banned, he and his mates still managed to get to the World Cup. 'When we went to France right… [we] walked through Calais customs and they took our passports and wouldn't let us through and about an hour later they come back and goes "all right".' Some wonder there was trouble in France. Many of the banned hooligans made it to the World Cup without much difficulty, despite a wide range of apparent measures designed to stop them.

Word creeps along the train to our carriage that in order to avoid the police we are to get off at Stockport, just a stop from Manchester Piccadilly. I escape to the toilet and I flush repeatedly, drowning out any chance of the Millwall tribe hearing me calling up Paul to pick me up in Stockport for a change in secret camera kit and a strategy meeting. I come back and sit down. 'Get off in Stockport and get killed,' a Millwall fan says to general laughter. Lee, who is travelling up with me, glances at me and we laugh nervously. This firm's idea of entertainment is seriously warped. 'Good day out, three to four got stabbed and everything… fucking riot horses and all that bollocks got stabbed,' one of them tells me.

They talk about the prospects for violence kicking off today. It seems inevitable that there will be at the very least a confrontation in Stockport. It's not that there is the scent of trouble – that's the actual plan. I head off to change out of the covert gear before there is trouble on the way to or at Maine Road, the Manchester City ground. I re-converge with Millwall at Piccadilly station and begin the heavily policed march to the match. There was trouble earlier in the season when Manchester City travelled to Millwall. Today, rightly, the police are taking no chances.

Ian Payne, who is a friend of Nightmare's and who I first met on the trip to Leicester, creeps up on me as we march in convoy with 3,000 of Millwall.

'Oi, Macca. You're game for a ruck anywhere, mate,' he whispers into my ear as the police horses shoo us into line. They bump against some of the fans. If you are with animals, you half-expect to be treated like an animal.

'Get fucking in line,' the policeman says.

Payne leans into me again. I take a long drag on my fag, still not able to inhale.

'We got a top firm here, the best in years, mate. If it kicks off here, it will go down in history.' That is why some football fans are treated like animals. And that is why sometimes they deserve to be treated like animals. If they weren't caged and hemmed in and have their civil liberties handcuffed on Saturday afternoons, there is no telling the anarchy and damage that would rain down upon towns and cities the length and breadth of the country. I end my conversation with Payne, agreeing with him happily on the prospect of mayhem.

'Are you Millwall then?' I am asked by someone else.

'No, mate,' I say, with an expression that is half-frown, half-smirk, 'I'm here by invitation, if you know what I mean.' It is understood. He shows me respect by nodding his approval.

One Millwall fan is frank about his intentions and tells a police-woman, 'If it kicks off, we will kick it off. If you leave us alone and let us go and watch the match, then we're sweet. There's no singing, no violence, is there? But if we bump into... Man City, they're going to get it.'

Another talks to me about the City Governors, Manchester City's gang of hooligans.

'They've [away teams] been battered to fuck up here, all of them... This is different, though, ain't it? This is a pukka little firm as well... This is like... the old days.' He is reminiscing but it is menacing because I know it is going to kick off. My language is foul today. Bad language is the hooligan's syntax, but today I am joining in with relish. It also is an indicator of my stress levels.

We get to the ground and eventually Lee and I decide not to go in. During the game I can see Danny on the terraces through a gap in the stadium structure. He is hooded and standing still. There is a public announcement asking home and away supporters to ignore some fighting on the terraces. There is clearly serious violence erupting in the ground. Police vans pull up and we move away.

When the match ends, the Millwall supporters are kept in the ground while the Manchester City supporters riot outside the ground. The violence from Marseilles has just been transposed to the streets of Manchester. I do a piece to camera into Lee's body camera. I look odd staring at his chest but no one notices because there are bricks flying about. (Afterwards I view the tapes. I look as tense as I have ever looked in the field. Much more so than when I was trounced in Copenhagen. We also have a video cameraman there, who is seen by the police getting into the BBC's rented Mercedes being driven by Paul. This has serious implications for us later on.)

We are marched back with the Millwall supporters. The streets are full. Students open their windows and are heckled at. A young woman appears, curious, at a window. 'Get your tits out for the lads,' they chant at her. It is a huge police operation. We are marched back to the station while transport is arranged. There is not enough room on the first train and another train is due out soon, so about 3,000 Millwall are encircled by police outside the station. I retreat to the back and ask to leave, persuading a police-man that it is a free country and I am entitled to exit the throng to go to eat. He lets me and Lee go. What he doesn't realize is that I have spent all day being a Millwall hooligan and now want out. The day is nearly over, but I need a break.

13th February 1999

In a pub off Leicester Square I meet the new generation of football hooligans, who seem to be more aware of the law and the police than the older generation. It's just a social call to the new breed of hooligan – a brand who have been apprenticed to some of the country's most malicious and dangerous football thugs. The investigation has taken a new turn. Using Jason's connections we seek out new targets and expand our tentacles further into the hooligan field. Danny, fresh from the march and the Millwall game, leads the new recruits.

The Reading Youth are at the core of the Chelsea and the Reading joint enterprise arrangement. The firms travel with each other and share the same prejudices and hatred. That's what alliances are about – shared prejudices. Danny is unbelievably friendly towards me. He has seen me at the Oxford vs Chelsea game, on the frontline at the Bloddy Sunday commemoration march and at Millwall. Those sightings, and the patronage of two Head-hunters, make a difference.

He turns to a friend and introduces us. 'These are my good mates and I love these lot.' He may be going over the top. I attribute this to the cocaine he tells me he's had. 'I'm off my head,' he says, as he strokes his shoulder-length hair. He has the longest hair of any hooligan I know. He proves himself on the terraces, I suppose, so he does not have to conform completely to the stereotype of the hooligan.

I am keen for this to be a quick hit and want to keep my time with Danny to a minimum. He is keen for us to spend the evening with him. 'Stay out with us, you'll love it. We'll have a right crack.'

Danny is keen to keep me up to date on the terrace trouble at the Manchester City–Millwall match. He says he went into the home team's end and started pulling up seats and throwing them at Man City supporters – 'Just ripping up seats and going mental... we

climbed in their end... just hitting them with chairs and throwing batteries and coins.' There is no blaming the other side. He says that the
Millwall firm he was travelling with started it. He says it proudly.

The young generation of hooligans is using new technology to
spread the word. They tell me that they have made their own video,
with personal interviews and footage from court cases and news
reports of their greatest hooligan highlights.

'Where do you get all the action from?'

'It's all police videos and that.'

'So, where do you get the police videos from?' I ask.

'You get them when you get arrested and that.'

His friends tell me it starts with the boys going to fight to the
music of The Verve's 'Bittersweet Symphony'. 'All the Reading walking down towards the Oxford ground, it's fucking mental, innit?'

I put in a heavily disguised journalistic request. 'Bring it down,
bring it down, mate. We'll put it on... and have a few beers.'

15th February 1999

The fake magazine cover is back from the designers. Daniele is by
popular demand on the front and only page of *Polkadot*. He is there
because I need to speak to him more than I need to speak to any of
the other PRs. It's time to board the fashion merry-go-round again.

16th February 1999

Memo: 16.2.99

From: Programme Legal Advice

To: Donal Mac Intyre

Subject: R vs Moonsinghe

'As you know, counsel for the prosecution have agreed to ask the
court to permit you to give evidence from behind a screen and they
are reasonably optimistic that that will succeed. The police have

agreed to smuggle you in and out of the court to reduce the risk of you being spotted. A barrister has been lined up by us to make an application to the court requesting that your identity be protected when you give evidence at the trial. As we have discussed, it is difficult to predict the outcome of this application (they are fairly rare) but we have asked counsel to give us a view on this.

'It appears that there is to be no pre-trial hearing to sort out these matters, so it is intended that both these applications be made on the first day of trial, which we understand is scheduled first of March...'

This is virgin legal territory and it will be interesting to see if a judge is willing to give an undercover journalist the same protective umbrella that he would give an undercover policeman. That, effectively, is what our legal team will be asking. I have not heard any more on the death-threat investigation. However, the BBC is conducting a security assessment on me to see if I need additional protection.

I phone Daniele in NY Elite today. He was not at the office because New York is hosting the fashion world right now and he is out and about. I try him on his mobile. He greets me in his best New York accent, acquired since the New Year. He is very comfortable with me and says that he wants to see his face on the magazine cover. 'The first of many,' I say. The point of the call is to get his patronage in order for me to talk to others when I'm in Milan and to ensure his ego will encourage him and them to meet me for another full and frank discussion.

Switching to another chair, I phone Ian Payne in Reading and arrange to meet. Filming myself with a small video camera, I change clothes before making the call. I don't change for visuals, but to psyche myself into the role. Believe who you are and so will others. You are what you wear – or at least I am.

As well as making important calls, I also receive one – from Manchester Police. They have traced the rented Mercedes to the

BBC and want to know if we have any relevant footage of what went on outside Manchester City's ground. We agree to get back to them. We will, of course, co-operate, but there are serious matters at stake. It is difficult to imagine us remaining with the football story if the police know exactly who is in the field and what we are investigating. This is one for the lawyers.

17th February 1999

I go to bed the same way I wake up – with a stress headache. I'll just have a coffee to help me sleep.

23rd February 1999

When fashion and football collide I have to learn to discriminate my 'ciaos' from my 'alwights'. Tonight there is the extraordinary Alexander McQueen show. Colin is filming me around London Fashion Week and we go to McQueen to get some high-fashion pictures. What a show, and what a contrast to tomorrow's adventure – the continuing courtship of my hooligan friends. I am going from high fashion to low farce.

24th February 1999

'Alwight, mate?' I ask, invoking my stock phrase.

'Alwight, Macca.' Ian 'Payney' Payne greets me in similar fashion. He and his friend are on their way to Bristol Crown Court and I am trusted enough to give them a lift. I can't believe it. Eight months ago I was Little Bo Peep in this environment and now I hold my own in conversation with the hardest of these nutcases. This is a major advance for me. Today, I have two of my own little firm with me, Mike and Lee, both dressed in the requisite thug uniform. Each is carefully positioned to get the best camera positions for our two court-bound comrades. I am driving and whenever my conversation slackens they chime in to rescue me or to thread a line of conversation that is evidential or just plain interesting.

On the way down, Payney and his mate are still slightly guarded with me. We (the team) prod and probe, making some headway, but our passengers are not giving full and frank disclosure. The boys are up in court for violence at a Bristol Rover vs Reading match last year.

DONAL: 'So they don't have it all on video, presumably?'
            [Some fighting has been caught on video, but not all.]

PAYNEY: 'Not all of it, they ain't got me doing hardly nothing on video. They got me walking out of the pub with a fucking metal tray and a fucking beer bottle in the other hand, that's all they got me doing. So I'll try and get a little explanation for that.'

DONAL: 'Like what? Any ideas?'

PAYNEY: 'I got arrested the week before, and I felt that I had to get out of the area as quickly as possible, and I felt I had to arm myself.'

DONAL: 'Just in case?'

PAYNEY: 'Just in case there was any of them Bristol hooligans outside.'

DONAL: [In a mock judge's accent] 'Mr Payne, what did you do with the aforementioned weapons outside the pub?'

PAYNEY: 'Sold them to the highest bidder...'

He is referring to a brawl that he describes as 'a show of strength'. He and his friend are up for violent disorder. The friend doesn't talk in too much detail about the case.

FRIEND: 'One of the witness statements says a man in light-coloured trousers and a light-coloured baseball hat appeared from the pub with a heavy chair, chased a man down the street and set about him.'

DONAL:	'Was that you?'
FRIEND:	'I don't know… I'm not saying nothing.'
DONAL:	[In mickey-taking accent] 'I am not prepared to say.'
FRIEND:	'I don't know you as well as Payney does.'

I have been recommended as an 'all right geezer,' but he has to see the whites of my eyes before he will fully trust me. I try and put him at ease, saying, 'That's all right, no problem, no problem, it's all right, business is business.'

I negotiate a few more roundabouts and in a roundabout way extract a couple more stories before I drop them off about five minutes from the courthouse. I park the car up and rig up the camera with a fresh tape for the homeward journey. Then my bogus firm and I go for coffee and a chill out. I congratulate my team for fine work. It is massively stressful, but they make it look easy.

The day is not yet done – far from it. This afternoon I fly to Milan for the Italian fashion capital's annual spring soirée of *haute couture*. I make a mental note to eliminate my bad language. I have started a sin bin for every expletive and already owe a small fortune to the *Big Issue*, the beneficiary of my swearing. The team has promised to blow the whistle on my foul football language, but it's easier said than done: when Pip viewed tapes for the edit he found his own, normally pristine received pronunciation being contaminated by osmosis. He now owes a small fortune to the homeless as well.

The aim of this visit to Milan is to talk further to Daniele, and to track down Gérald Marie in order to renew our friendship and ignite the investigation.

25th February 1999

While I'm covering fashion in Milan, I receive some advice from the BBC lawyers:

Memo: 25.2.99
From:.   Programme Legal Advice
Subject: Donal Mac Intyre

'Further update on the current situation: As you know the trial in which Donal is scheduled to give evidence is due to start on Monday, the first of March. We've been in touch with the prosecution barrister and are endeavouring to persuade him to present the application for us as, we feel it will carry more weight with the judge if the prosecution did it. However, if he is unwilling, then we will do it ourselves... The application will now be made on Tuesday the second because of our counsel's commitments on Monday the first, but we have an undertaking from the prosecution that they will not raise Donal's name in court until after the (BBC's) application on Tuesday.'

The threat is very real. The case is to be heard just four miles from where the heart of the football investigation is based. We must be extremely careful. A misplaced photograph or court report could mean the end of football and other investigations in the UK this year.

26th February 1999

In the nightclub called Shocking, Lino is having a crisis. His cocaine has either been stolen or he has forgotten where he has hidden it in the club. I'm a bit cynical and suggest he may have consumed it last night, but he is adamant that he had it in the club this morning. Apparently, it is a sizeable amount of high-grade Brazilian cocaine.

'[There is] still the shit of the Brazilian [referring to the mule who smuggled it into the country] on it. It's like there's three plastic to take it off.' Concern and distress is written on his face.

'So was that really good Brazilian coke?', I inquire naively.

Lino gives me a look of understatement. 'Oooooooo,' he enunciates with pursed lips. 'It's pure... it's really pure... With one of that you can make three times with the cut... we going to make a line together.' I don't think that is an offer. I think it is a statement of fact for when he finds the cocaine. But I don't think any more about it. I'm supposed to be a drug dealer in the football story, but such junctions always put me on edge. I've been faced with this situation before in other investigations and the rule is to act in one of three ways: go to the police and hand them over, destroy them, or send them off for testing and then destroy them.

Tonight an English camera crew came to the club. They were doing a holiday feature for British television on Milan's nightlife. Before the crew leaves, Lino takes them aside and tells them, pointing at me, that I am 'the best photographer in London'. The crew don't believe him. They know me better than that. Much better.

27th February 1999

Life seems to be turning full circle. I am back to football, only this time in Italy. I just can't get away from the beautiful game. We want to take some of our friends to Juventus vs Inter Milan at the magnificent San Siro stadium to see if a little bit of sport will relax them into further self-incrimination. I start with a full cast list of possibilities and end up with Lino and his girlfriend.

Lino arranges to collect me at The Principe, the hotel I'm staying at. He and his girlfriend have a scooter and I am going to follow them to the match by taxi. But when Lino arrives, he wants to come up to my room. I'm not quite sure what he wants, but I kind of go along with it. It's all right anyway, I tell myself, because the room has two cameras and I am wearing a body rig.

I should have expected it. We get into the room and Lino goes straight to the mirrored wardrobe. 'Ahhhhhh, oh no, it's the Brazilian cocaine,' I say to myself. 'Shit.' (Doesn't count for the swearbox because I say it in my head.) I realize Lino is going to expect me to take cocaine with him and I panic. This could blow the entire gig. It's the most flustered I've been undercover that I can remember. The minute I see the 'Charlie', as my football friends call it, I start to back-peddle and then rush around the room secretly turning on the covert cameras.

Lino starts to cut cocaine on the wardrobe. He says he brought it up so we can have a line together. He is very insistent. It is his attempt at personal bonding. I go through a list of desperate and pitiful excuses.

'I don't want to have this now, I want to save this for a specific purpose. I'll tell you that later [when I can think of one].' When this doesn't work I fumble a few more: 'I've a had bad blast last night', 'I want to take some away with me because I want to save it for later', 'I had a really bad comedown'.

'You're going to love it. I want to do it with you,' Lino insists. He starts to snort through a rolled-up bank note. I change tack. 'No, no, I'm going to save it for later. I'm glad you didn't lose it. That was nearly 2 grams down the bloody swanney.' He challenges me and corrects me – 'It was 12 grams' – and is appalled when I start to scrape the cocaine meant for me with my hand into a piece of paper. Concerned that I'm ruining it, he neatly scrapes it into a proper line and packs it away for me and hands it over.

We leave the room. I have my little wrap of high-grade cocaine. Terror. I am in a foreign country with an amount that would send me to jail. Since I can't go to the police and hand it over or send it off for testing and then have it destroyed, I aim to destroy it myself. I go down the stairs with Lino and see him and his girlfriend onto their scooter, then race to the loo with my contraband. It's time to get down on my knees in front of the toilet. I feel like a drunken teenager.

There aren't many broadcasters who do a whispered piece to camera with their head over a toilet bowl. I unwrap the cocaine in front of the body camera. I lift the toilet seat. I flush and watch the cocaine go down into Milan's waste system. I rub my hands together flicking the last grains of cocaine into the water. For full compliance I go to the sink and wash my hands rigorously to clean them of all traces of the substance. I leave for the game, trying to remind myself that this is fashion and not football – no Chelsea, no bad language.

28th February 1999

There is a lot of police activity outside and inside the hotel. I am getting worried. Just down from my room there are four well-dressed men in the *Miami Vice* sense, only with an Italian flavour. I walk past wearing my secret camera kit. I act normal. We are all puzzled by what's going on. Our camera crew, who are shooting general views around Milan, are filming outside the hotel and the police move them on.

Things are looking very dim. Has my cover been blown or am I just being paranoid? I quiz a waiter and the picture becomes clear. My room neighbour, so close he's nearly my room-mate, is a minister in the Italian government and the well-dressed men are his bodyguards. They are here for a few days – that's the end of inviting anyone to my room for now. More worrying still is that every day, every few hours, I am going to have to walk past them wearing a secret camera kit which, at the first-glance search of an x-ray, could look like a bomb. While they're around, I'll have to put the kit on outside the hotel.

The best-dressed bodyguards in the world look, peruse and sniff. Upon reflection they look better dressed than I do when I am playing the role for the 419 fraud investigation. I must take notes. They are bored, predictably so. I walk past with the camera bag and am viewed with suspicion. I wave my key and head towards the lift, aware of their eyes following me. They're doing their job, I'm doing mine. All is well.

Keeping up appearances I attend the Gianfranco Ferré show. I have no interest in it at all, not in the clothes or the models or the glamour. Having seen the dark and seedy side of fashion, very little in this world touches or interests me now. I am immune to it. I am late because of the minister's well-dressed guards. I run out of film, which is just as well because it's only a waste of processing. I continue to flash the camera anyway.

Every day I try to catch up with Daniele to show him the photographs I've taken of him and to try to get another chat. He is so busy that he can't see me. He is working all day and partying all night.

I try to get permission to photograph at Versace but they have not heard of *Polkadot* magazine. In fact they call it '*Polkapop*' magazine. I agree that it's a much better title and vow to try and persuade the fictitious editor to change the name immediately.

1st March 1999

It's Monday and it's Milan. The team meet in a little café called Richard's, close to the Fiera Milano, a big exhibition centre much like Earl's Court, which is hosting the Moda de la Fashion (Milan Fashion Week). The little café has become our unofficial office. Colin is trying to manage my tiredness and my coffee obsession. Heaven is twenty cups a day. It is getting out of hand, especially since I discovered a *macchiato*, a small espresso with a dash of milk. For me, Milan is not the centre of fashion, but the capital of caffeine.

Again, the tentative calls to Daniele fail to elicit a decent response and he keeps putting me off. I wonder if he has smelled a rat. When you're undercover, if things don't go your way or start to go askew, you try to analyse the worst-case scenario and then backtrack. There are still a couple of days before he goes to Paris and then back to New York. Colin feels Daniele must be genuinely busy because otherwise he would want to see his photograph. The photograph has now been made into a mocked-up front cover and looks like a reasonable copy of a dummy issue. He will be impressed when he sees it. Fortunately, it's the only half-passable shot I took in six months of being a pseudo-photographer.

This one evening sees the dénouement of a ruse that has been months in the preparation, all to engineer a 'chance' meeting between Gérald Marie of Elite and me. Our very own sports journalist, 'K' (part of the BBC team), has arranged to interview 'the G man', as we now call him, under the pretext of writing a feature on sportsmen and fashion. I will turn up at the venue and accidentally bump into them. Colin brings K and we spend a tense afternoon choreographing our roles more thoroughly than any ballet dancers.

The meeting has been arranged directly with Gérald by phone. I warn K that Gérald may be late, but in fact he's early. They sit together on a platform level with the bar in a hotel lounge, the same hotel I'm staying at. I sit in the far corner across a crowded room. I can't hear their conversation but the plan is that I interrupt the interview to make a short, polite intervention, enough to set a marker but nothing too pushy.

It sounds easy enough, but I am a stress bunny. This intervention could be one of the most important in the investigation. I bungle it with racing nerves, fumbling my words and talking too quickly. Somehow the sense gets across. Gérald is clearly pleased to see me and tries to keep me at the table. After about thirty minutes I get up. We share a few jokes and he asks me, elliptically, if I am going to 'the Temple' (his name for the whorehouse). We make a loose arrangement to meet there the following evening. When I am gone, K asks Gérald if I am Mac, the photographer. He says, 'Yes'. She goes on to garland my career with fantastic credits to raise my standing in Gérald's eyes.

Mission accomplished.

My coup with Gérald isn't the only success story today. In the afternoon I get a call on my mobile as I'm sipping yet more coffee. It is from New Scotland Yard. The detective who phones is part of Operation Kitson, the unit that has been investigating the allegations originating from my *World In Action* programme. He informs me that Mr Susantha Moonesinghe, who had been organizing the bogus weddings, has pleaded guilty so there is no need for me to appear as a witness. It's a huge relief that I won't have to testify and risk exposing my cover. I have no idea what this means for the threats emanating from the investigation. I hope this has eased the safety concerns, though I know it's the price you have to pay for doing this kind of work.

2nd March 1999

I can't sleep. Hotel rooms have become my life and MTV and CNN my close friends. Today, I continue my fruitless trail to Daniele and to Gérald, who I am supposed to ring to confirm our playboy get-together. I can't reach him on the phone. I go to Williams 'whorebar' in the hope of meeting him, but he does not show. I get worried that I have missed a vital opportunity to get to know him better.

3rd March 1999

Today, I bump into Diego in the Grand Fiera. He kisses me on both cheeks (it's all right, I have thirty pieces of silver in my pocket). My elbows, as usual, protect my rib cage from human contact because of the covert equipment. He says he wants to anoint me as an honorary Moonsinner. I am surprised and delighted. I have achieved one of my aims insofar as it makes it easier for me to travel through this transient international community. I am going to be one of the élite Milanese nightclub fraternity. After all those thousands of hours bonding, caressing egos, nurturing contacts and sowing seeds, I have broken into the brotherhood. Diego fills in the details. 'To become one of the boys, you have to receive the *Iniziazione*.'

'The initiation ceremony?' I query, wondering what this entails and dreading some awful sexual ceremony.

'Yes. Mine was in the back of Shocking.' Diego laughs, recalling his own initiation. 'Oliver with the stick of a broom, you got like me sitting on my knees [he gets up and gestures a knighting action] and all the boys around and Oliver was like, "In the name of the moon, I make you an official sinner". And after that they were all like kicking me and beating me up.'

I try to appear delighted and humbled by my imminent beatification.

'Yeah, we're going to beat you up,' Diego returns. I try to envisage this – it's not a pretty picture. I can't believe that I am volunteering to be beaten up by a group of Italian playboys. I mean, you'd swear I was a football hooligan. I put a brave face on it. 'So you're going to initiate me as a Moonsinner. Fantastic.'

'We're going to beat you up on Wednesday night in Shocking.'

At least that's something to look forward to. I can't wait. 'Don't worry,' Diego reassures me, 'we won't beat you too hard because you are bigger than me.' He laughs merrily and tells me where to go to collect my special Moonsinners ring, a badge as relevant to this world as my tattoo is for the Head-hunters.

After this triumph, I try to pin down Gérald again before we depart for Paris. He tells me that he's going to be in the hotel gym and sauna around five o'clock. I say I might see him there. The venue poses a problem for me, though – nowhere to hide the covert equipment! Still, I need to cultivate this friendship, so it's all grist to the mill. I arrive on time. Gérald is late. I am sitting in the Jacuzzi and he winks at me as he goes into the steam room. I stay put – I don't want to appear to be too much in his face. It's probably an unnecessary concern because the fashion world operates very much 'in your face'. After fifteen minutes I follow him into the steam room and he, in avuncular fashion, tells me to put some flip-flops on to prevent '*champignons*'. I guess he is referring to athlete's foot fungus, or mushrooms, as I translate it in my pheasant French.

Gérald says that he had fun in the Temple the other day and was sorry I couldn't share the experience (it transpires he had forgotten about our arrangement). Later, in the pool, his friend and business partner, Roberto Caan, joins us and they speak in French, a language that is beyond me. We all leave together after doing a few lengths and I nervously suggest a boys get-together afterwards for the Inter Milan vs Manchester United game, as it's on television. There is no need to be stressed. Gérald is very partial to the idea and invites me to his suite to watch it.

Before we leave the locker room, Gérald, childlike, admires the hotel robes that are left in the changing room for guests. With much good humour, he stuffs three or four robes and a couple of pairs of complementary flip-flops inside his own robe and sneaks it all off to his room. I fall about laughing. He looks like the Michelin man.

We meet up later at the hotel bar. I order a Sea Breeze (vodka, grapefruit juice and cranberry juice) – it's fashion after all. Gérald, who refuses to accept any hospitality from me, has a problem with the bill. He sorts it out and we walk up to his room. I jump out at my floor to change tapes and say I'll meet them up there shortly. I am racing around like a lunatic to get my stuff together but trying to be chilled. That's what the part demands. I behave so differently with Gérald compared to the PRs. With them, I have a high-octane, brash personality, but with Gérald I am more subdued. I still feel that I haven't got the confidence to lend any humour to our relationship. He may be reading my soft tread as enigmatic. Be that as it may, it's working, so I won't fix what isn't broken.

Gérald's hotel suite is expansive. I'm made to feel welcome. Cannabis and beer are offered around the room, with Gérald rolling up the spliffs. He knows his football. His business partner, Roberto, knows his football, too. Describing the need for a stout defence, he labels the black footballers 'niggers'. He repeats it twice. Gérald does not blink, though he most certainly hears this. Among the models, these two men represent black supermodel Naomi Campbell. I can't imagine that she would be best pleased to hear her agents speaking like this. I refuse another offer of a joint, preferring, I intimate, to concentrate on the beer, and rev up the football testosterone chat.

Our schedule for the rest of the evening is dinner and then the 'whorehouse'. The restaurant we go to is an old haunt of Gérald's. We are taken there in a chauffeur-driven Mercedes. As ever, Gérald is the centre of attention. He commands such regard because he is charismatic and entertaining, if not a little risqué. He regales the assembled company with tales of Viagra-and-cocaine cocktails he has tried, and chides and scolds and makes fun of everyone at the table.

While Gérald discusses his divorce from Linda Evangelista, I have to answer Roberto's questions about my career in photography. 'I hear you are very good at portrait,' he says. I demur modestly, but he presses the point. I let the conversation fizzle out, but he suggests I talk to Gérald about some work. I say I am too busy already and if the schedule gets any tighter, my quality will suffer.

We go on to the 'whorehouse'. Williams offers clients an escort service – company that you pay for and that you can pay to take home with you. There is a gallery of women to choose from. Some are dancers and prostitutes and some are just prostitutes. One girl, who was initially turned away from the table by Gérald shouting within earshot, 'She's fat, she's fat', talks to me. She is from Romania and is supporting her family back home by working the punters at this strange art deco establishment. Gérald takes control and takes a good deal of time before he takes his pick. It's time to make my excuses and leave. Colin is sitting opposite me on his own, playing the sad-lonely-punter-looking-at-a-bit-of-flesh role, but in fact is filming Gérald and me. I claim a headache. I joke that I must be the only person in Milan who goes to a whorehouse and gets a headache. Gérald is too busy even to notice me depart.

4th March 1999

I locate Gérald again in the morning, when I drift down to the lobby of our hotel. He is paying his bill and is off home with his coterie of business colleagues for the start of Paris Fashion Week. I shake his hand and we agree to meet there on Sunday or Monday. He glides through the revolving doors carrying his luggage, pauses and looks back, pursing his lips. He is blowing me a hands-free kiss. I think he likes me. I have no idea why. Sporting chat is clearly a rare commodity in Gérald's circle. His two friends smile in my direction. If I am Gérald's friend, then I am theirs by proxy. I am anointed.

There is another annointment awaiting me. I don't know it yet but Diego wants to ennoble me as a Moonsinner tonight. He is with a new girlfriend – Carolyn Park, a leading model – in her hotel and invites me over for a beer. They are both stoned when I get there, but Carolyn has a fashion show shortly and is trying to get in shape for it. I remember that Carolyn appeared in the first Alexander McQueen show I saw. She looks so different now.

Fortunately, the beating seems superfluous to Diego's personal interpretation of the initiation ceremony. In any case, there is no broom available to beat me with. Silently, I thank God. It's not the pain that I'm worried about, it's the embarrassment. Diego calls us to order. I stand for the coronation. 'OK, guy[s], this is an important celebration. I know you never worked for a club, and I know that you never participated officially to the contest, but because you have shown great heart towards me and Oliver... Which finger you prefer?'

'Put it on here.' My middle finger is offered. 'So I'm an honorary Moonsinner now.' Diego gives me a hug in full Italian fashion. 'What does that allow me to do?' I inquire, curious about my newfound rights and responsibilities. I turn to the mirror and film my reflection, flashing the ring.

Diego answers happily. 'Everything. Now you can go down to the receptionist, open your pants [Diego pulls his pants down] like this and walk around like this. This is what the ring allows you to do.' He elaborates further on my rights. He says that I can walk into a church and snort coke at the altar while the priest is concelebrating mass. 'The moon is your sin,' he advises enigmatically.

5th March 1999

One of the newest and most successful model agencies in Milan is Paolo Tomei's. Paolo, a former male model and booker, is big, hearty and open. His offices are swish and smart with orange designer furniture. I meet Paolo ostensibly to discuss photographing him for my (bogus) exhibition of fashion. Really, I want to get his honest view of the business and the dangers that exist for the girls who enter it. If I declared myself as a journalist, I would be unlikely to get an unadulterated perspective.

I prop myself up in a chair, careful that my tee-shirt cam is not obscured by the high table we're seated at. As ever in Milan, the smokes are out and everyone's puffing away, me included, though still somehow managing to look convincing enough without inhaling. I take a few photographs. Paulo tells me that the English girls are really popular in Milan. And there is a never-ending supply of new English girls. He takes his book of models and deals them as if playing snap. 'English, English, English,' he repeats as he trawls through the deck of models' cards.

He says that in England the designers accept new faces but in Milan they are more reluctant to push unknowns to stardom. But even for those models whose star shines brightly in the fashion world, longevity is not guaranteed.

'You take three months to become a star today; max six months maybe you're gone [he waves his arm as if discarding litter and smiles ironically]. Not so easy to be up for five or six years. They use up and then they throw away.'

Paulo deals with London-based agencies who send their models to Milan. It seems surprising that the London agencies don't know the dangers that can await young models out there. I ask him a leading question, though thankfully he doesn't see it as such: 'Do you find drugs a problem?'

'...Lots of the models are involved with drugs... All the fashion business is...' I can't believe that he is not aware of the devastating portrait he is painting of his industry. The shoot is finished and I promise to discuss the photographs with him during Paris Fashion Week.

Lisa talks to one of Paolo's bookers as part of her on-going research and it is quite apparent that some of Paolo's staff know the PRs' *modus operandi*, but don't do anything to prevent their models getting involved in that world. This is one of the conversations that proves that many working in the agencies know what goes on:

BOOKER:	'Milan can be dangerous, especially for models. Because of this PR always around them.'
LISA:	'Sorry, PR?'
BOOKER:	'Of discos and clubs, you know? They want to take the models down to their clubs, so...'
LISA:	'The PRs, sorry, what's that?'
BOOKER:	'The PR of the clubs, like Hollywood [and]

Shocking. They go and look for models to take down to the club so that all the other people go in the same club because they know that there are models there. I know that when they are young, they start drinking, smoking, using drugs... We can't control them when we are in the office, we don't know where they are, especially at night – you don't have time to stay with them twenty-four hours.'

LISA: 'It must be a huge responsibility for you. It must be very stressful.'

BOOKER: 'It is. Well we tend to consider the girls, now, like not human – sometime I find myself treating them like they are goods to sell. I forget that they are human. So sometime you don't call them every night and you don't really take good care of them, and you find out they [stay] out until four o'clock in the morning and they have to work the next day...
'I'm sure a lot of girls do use drugs, I'm sure they do. I saw last night, they were all drunk, but that's okay, it was a party, you know?'

The girls the booker is referring to, by his own account, are as young as thirteen years of age.

6th March 1999

No matter what hands of friendship are extended, there is never a moment when I feel a kinship or sympathy for the PRs. Something always reminds me just how sordid and disgusting this whole scene is. I am reminded why young models should never be allowed near these people and why I am doing this story. Today is one of those days.

Diego, in relaxed and open mood, is chatting to me in the hotel lobby. I take advantage of the opportunity and pursue a line of questions that would normally provoke camouflage and evasion.

DONAL:	What was the youngest girl you went to bed with, you know, as a Moonsinner. And how did they handle it?'
DIEGO:	'Honestly, fifteen.'
DONAL:	'Honestly?'
DIEGO:	'I was eighteen, she was fifteen.'
DONAL:	'How did she handle it?'
DIEGO:	'It was a fuck. It was just a fuck, because anyway she was fifteen... I could not hang out with her but I didn't care. Anyway I got my six points, and she wanted that... At the time I really didn't felt like I give a fuck, even how old she was. I was fine. I was fine with whatever was happening.'

I can't tell if Diego actually regrets this or if now, as then, he couldn't care less. Sometimes, however, even Diego does have some insight into his behaviour and that of his friends. He recounts one time when he brought a sixteen-year-old model to a party:

'I've been at parties which a girl sixteen years old stands naked in the middle of the bath and ten men jerk off around her. And she is pleased with it, she [is] actually... Me, I slept with her two weeks before, and [I] look at this, and I don't stop [the guys] because I have no right to say, "Guys, stop, what the fuck are you doing?" because I am the one who take her to parties normally. And she came to the house with me, and half the men are my friends, and the other half I know them...'

'Is that what happened. Did that happen?' I say softly.

He confirms with a tepid grunt. 'Uh-huh. She has been asking for it, but when I see, like, ten [men] coming on a baby, in that vulgar way, their not even giving her pleasure, that's like using a person.'

There is nothing to be done. Milan is Milan and Diego feels that whatever he says or does, nothing will change. Even with the drugs he says, 'If I don't offer first coke to a fifteen-year-old girl...someone else would do that.' He has said to me before, 'I know you think I'm an animal, but I am trying my best.' I really hope he is changing.

This is the last day of Milan Fashion Week and after meeting Diego I've got to dash to the airport to catch a flight to London (tomorrow I revert to the world of football). One of the last comments that Diego makes is more perceptive than he realizes. 'I remember when I saw you first, you look fresh and young, now you look like an old man. What have you been doing, man?'

'You don't know the half of it, Diego, you don't know the half of it,' I say.

I arrive in London at about 10.30p.m., but immediately have to prepare for filming tomorrow.

7th March 1999

It's a wake-up call for 6.00a.m. I head for Heathrow to catch the 8.30a.m. shuttle to Manchester. It has a number of football fans on it. I keep a low profile. Paul – who travelled up with Jason yesterday – is there to pick me up. I am due to make contact with The Penguin this morning after some strong coffee. The plan is for me to stay over in Manchester tonight (Sunday) to meet some of Jason's friends. On Monday, Jason is travelling with me down to London in the team car. The Merc has now been replaced full-time with the Land-Rover, which is wired for pictures. I have to be in London by four o'clock on Monday because I am flying out to Paris for Fashion Week at five, but Jason, of course, doesn't know that. He is staying with some pals and I am staying in a hotel tonight, but Jason doesn't know that either. He thinks I'm staying with an ex-girlfriend.

We have no joy trying to link up with Jason before the Man United vs Chelsea match. The friends he is staying with are unhelpful and I can't work out whether they're just dim or whether he is trying to avoid me. Presumably the former, as we find Jason afterwards and he generously invites us to the equivalent of a hooligan's convention at a pub in Manchester, tacitly rubber-stamping our

Head-hunter credentials. There are hooligans from four of the country's biggest hooligan firms and there are two from the BBC's. The situation is highly dangerous and could turn volatile at any moment in company such as this.

We spend an hour there laughing at Jason's jokes – he is in command and directs the humour, as usual – and then leave, delivering our strong handshakes to the boys. We break into a dash for the car as soon as we're out of sight. To think, any one of them could have picked up a glass and stabbed us with it. That would not be unusual behaviour for them. One guy said to me, 'I even go to games when there is no violence.' Some concession.

It is apparent that we are a little excitable at the threat we've just escaped. Close call. Every encounter you survive is a relief, but this one would have been very nasty if a wire had accidentally come loose from my body-belt covert kit.

8th March 1999

I brace myself to drive Jason back to London. Paul tells Jason that I'm a bad driver. I hold my hand up and agree. 'Imagine, Paul telling you I'm a bad driver. I'm a self-confessed bad driver.'

'I'm a self-confessed bad passenger,' Jason replies, fast as a whippet.

The weather is overcast. We have a cup of tea before we leave Manchester and then I drive around the M56 and miss the turning for the M6 and come off in Runcorn towards Liverpool Airport. That's when I realize that a three-hour journey to London is going to take five hours.

It's a long time to be alone with a volatile and violent man. It's a long time for a tired man to talk without dropping himself in it. Luckily, though, Jason is in cosy humour. He is still celebrating the fact that a belch of hooligans congregated in his honour last night. 'Yeah, sweet. I met up with a load of others earlier, they'll come out, it's good, they come out on the beer to have a drink with me. The other guy who came out, come out from Chesterfield. That's 35 miles away.'

'That's respect,' I say. He agrees and I lard it on a bit more, knowing how he rejoices in the brotherhood accorded by these male bonding rituals. 'You know everybody, mate.'

It is true that Jason has a vast number of contacts, and not just in the hooligan fraternity either. He has many friends on the criminal spectrum and is keen to establish his hard-man credentials with me, a supposed international drug dealer. A posse of his friends have been nicked for drug smuggling. 'Six hundred and forty kilos of Charlie, a hundred bleeding grand's worth, 30 plus [years in prison], solicitor reckons. Top man might get 40 plus years.'

I start to pout and declare that I've never been nicked.

'Sweet one, I'd like to say the same thing. I [I'd] say me being nicked was my own doing, that's the regret of it... It was me own fucking stupidity, me own fault – drink and football.'

Jason is opening up. In the first stretch of the journey I gave part of my invented past to him and now he is delivering, quid pro quo.

'Yeah, at one time I was fucking looking at five or seven, GBH, section 18, violent disorder. Violent disorder is one up from affray...' he continues, clearly well versed on the legalities. 'It was just a pub brawl, but the man ended up in a coma and the [police] pointed the finger at me. But the man come out of the coma, it was just a pub brawl.'

'Good one,' I say encouragingly.

'I had a top brief,' he admits. 'The Old Bill fabricated evidence, they wanted me so much, they fabricated evidence. They lied too many times and my brief caught them out. If they hadn't lied, if they'd stayed fair, I'd been away. I'd been away, no doubt about it.'

Jason has been lucky. As an organizer he has always managed, sometimes by sheer fluke, to avoid jail. But Jason and drink with a shot of football is lethal. 'I go on binges, proper binges, I can't see the point of having two or three, I can't do it anyway. Once I've had two or three, I get the taste for it and I want to like crack on... I think I may as well have a proper hangover. Bad way to think about it.'

At the heart of Jason's origin as a football thug is an experience he had as a fifteen-year-old. 'I went to Wolves, my mate asked me to hold this fucking Union Jack, I was only about fifteen or something and this bloke's gone, "What's on the flag, mate?" and I've gone, "Chelsea" and he's come over and gone to whack me. So I spat at him and I whacked him as hard as I could.'

Jason's attacker was a fully grown man but at fifteen Jason had had no fear. He got off on the adrenaline of the fight – and so began his career as a thug.

Through violence he seeks respect – the need for it extending to his funeral. He says his friends tell him that, whenever he goes, there'll be a big turnout.

At long last the journey comes to an end. I am exhausted at the concentration required to keep it tight. Jason tests me and probes and unfortunately remembers and files everything in the back of his mind. This is the danger. I exchange millions of words with him and have to ensure that one sentence or misplaced phrase or line does not raise suspicions. I drop him off at his car and exhale. There's not a lot of time to draw breath, though. Next stop the airport and back on the Mac attack again. Paris calls.

9th March 1999

I arrange to meet Daniele tonight, ostensibly to chat about the magazine cover. He believes that I need to take a couple more snaps for *Polkadot* magazine and knows that I need to get it done before he goes to New York. He is keen to get together but, as in Milan, he seems run off his feet. He is either suspicious of me or desperate to prove himself on his new promotion trail. Or it could be a bit of both.

Frustratingly, he blows me out again. I phone my other quarry, Gérald, and get the warmest of greetings – '*Hello*, dar-ling'. He promises to meet up later and tells me to call. I hate doing this bit, phoning him back. I worry that my constant calls will make him think me a pest. It is strange that of all the stressful situations and interaction that I go through in this job, it's social etiquette that seems to worry me the most. It's just the embarrassment of it all. Colin has to keep pushing me and finally, at midnight, when I make my third call in the last five hours, I get him. 'Ah Mac! C'est le Mac,' he says in an aside to a friend. We arrange to meet in Le Bain Douche at 1.30a.m. I have no confidence that Gérald will show and arrange to meet Diego and Carolyn there, too. It is a wise move.

Even though I don't meet Gérald, it is useful to touch base with Carolyn and Diego. They arrive at the club and come straight to my table. They make a bizarre and apparently sweet couple and seem very loving, although their relationship seems mainly to revolve around drug-taking. They do cocaine openly in the club. A chauffeur who is driving Carolyn to the shows this week indulges, too. Diego is spaced out, bumbling and spitting out incoherent sentences. He turns to his loved one and tenderly squeezes her hand.

'Mac, I'm fucked, I'm fucking fucked up,' he says. (That's a fortune for the sin bin, I think to myself.) Carolyn has been working all day and was up for a rehearsal at 5.00a.m. It's three o'clock in the morning and she hasn't slept in the last two nights. She leans onto my shoulder. 'This is me on 2 grams of coke and I'm falling asleep.'

'So how much do you need to keep you awake, 2 grams?' I ask.

'I nearly collapsed at the last show, so tired, all these people pulling at you,' she replies, unable to concentrate on the question. She turns her head constantly to view the fashion television monitor (with footage from all the shows) in the centre of the room to see if she appears.

While her cocaine habit is still furious, at least she has given up heroin, or smack as it is called on the street. I ask what made her stop. 'I nearly died,' she says. 'I nearly died, my best friend nearly died, my boyfriend nearly died. I figured, "What the fuck?"'

Diego explains that he has been advising Carolyn to cut back on her drug use. If you take a break after heavy drug use, you see drugs in a new perspective. He offers this opinion while he snorts cocaine that has been bought with Carolyn's fantastic earnings from the catwalk.

10th March 1999

Finally, arrangements are made to meet Daniele. I hope he is in the mood to talk. I go to the flat he is renting in the red-light district of Paris for a one-to-one. He is still rushing. There is slight panic in his voice and he appears uncomfortable, sitting on the edge of his sofa. I try to put him at ease by talking in and around fashion. I talk about something that would put him at ease: drugs. People in fashion live in a complete drug culture and so does Daniele, so it's not the direct conversational opener you might think, although I have to be careful not to expose my lack of experience with it. Despite living in a crack house for two months in the course of one investigation, it is difficult to talk the talk without having walked the walk – not an option, obviously.

'I hate the down, I have to stay home all the next day,' Daniele says. He had a bad time of it in Milan after taking a couple of grams, which was why I had difficulty setting up a meeting with him. He is embarrassed about this. I let him know it is not a problem.

'You should have said to me, "Look, Mac, I'm having a bit of a cocaine wipe-out, so chill out, pal, we'll meet up in Paris."'

Now that Daniele is sufficiently at ease, I start throwing conversational lines about the models and the PRs and then send a direct question his way: has he had sex with any of the models he was supposed to be looking after when he was an Elite chaperon? He does not appear suspicious of this and answers frankly.

'The last time I did it [I] was dating my girlfriend. She was living with me in my room... and [there] was another girl – she was living in the same apartment [the Elite residence for the under-eighteen models].'

'In the same apartment? At the same time?' Daniele nods. I press him further. 'One of the models?'

'Yes.'

'And what happened? Did they ever find out?'

'No, no – they never find out, because my girlfriend, she not even feel [hear] about it, and the other girl she was very quiet, she never say anything about it.'

'What was she like? Was she very pretty?'

'Yes, she was pretty – she was seventeen. She was like, 'All I want is sex. If you don't give it to me, then I'll just go and get it somewhere else.' For me it's okay, I got two. If she's not going to give it to me, then I go [to] the other one.'

This is a man who was supposed to be looking after and protecting the same young models, and seems to think his behaviour is entirely normal. I suppose the real question is why nobody in fashion seems to think otherwise.

My working day is not yet over. At 11.00p.m. I go to a fashion party at a venue just off the Champs Elysées. There are television cameras everywhere. Carolyn is there with Diego and a camera swoops on her like a homing pigeon. She is dressed Goth-like, all in black and pouts and performs for the lens, interrupting my conversation with her about her drug-taking. She is twenty years old and admits to having been on cocaine from the age of fifteen, as well as taking heroin for a time while a model. Isn't it funny, I say to her, that at the same time she was shooting up, 'heroin chic' – the washed-out, drug-addict look – was in? 'Talk about being in harmony with your business.'

'Yeah, I was totally in harmony, but then it all went full circle and I was like, "Oh, shit, I'd better get rid of the linen and the black, oh shit, I can see my career is going down, baby." That was fucked up, because I could see it coming... I was freaking out and they said, "Carolyn, you can't be Goth no more." I was like, "You can take the girl away from the Goth, but you can't take the Goth out of the girl." It's always there, mate... I'll still be evil.' She frequently loses the track of our conversation. She's had too many drugs.

Carolyn is a perfect example of what this industry can do to young models. Everyone I meet in the fashion world has similar stories to tell – has made mistakes and seen the same mistakes made. They all say that the girls are too young but no one seems to want to do anything about it, and the same pattern of abuse and entrapment is repeated. Needlessly, girls are drawn into drugs and addiction and no one is there to help them out of it.

11th March 1999

I am invited to Diego and Carolyn's hotel. I cross the city in a cab and phone up from the foyer. They insist that I go to their room. Reluctantly, I go. I find them still getting ready to go out. Carolyn has to call by her agency to get some money to pay for some drugs. She has already moved to a more downmarket hotel to budget for her massive consumption of narcotics. I am distinctly uncomfortable in their private room, it is just too intimate. I leave as soon as I can and say I'll wait downstairs for them.

Diego arrives first. At this stage, he and I can talk frankly to each other and I take advantage of the opportunity to challenge him about doing drugs with Carolyn. 'You're a bad influence, Diego.'

'Me, I'm the best thing that happened to this girl in, like, ten years... I tried to make her stop, I don't want her to do that much... once in a while [is all right], but if it [you do it] every day... first you waste money, and second – which is worst than the first one – you destroy yourself, you do your body harm.' It is not harming her career yet, but it could, Diego says, exhibiting genuine concern. 'It's giving her a bad reputation, they aren't going to push her because it is always a risk that she is not going to show up.'

We go on to a Chinese restaurant and I gently question Carolyn. Diego's patronage is strong, but even so, she doesn't quite know what to make of me. Her revelations about her drug use do not break any confidences because it is normal to talk about drugs in fashion. It is the fashion patois, the small talk that is part and parcel of any dinner-table discussion and morning-coffee chat. In this industry, everyone is either coming down or getting high.

I look Carolyn in the eye. 'You should get off the drugs over the long term, because it is a bad business. I know. I've been there. I pulled back.' This isn't true, but I've seen enough casualties of the drug culture from my time in a crack house to say it with conviction. It is probably fruitless, but I say it because it just might provoke her to reconsider her habit.

'Every day, it's a fight. I could do it, but in a different situation,' she says. 'With what I do and how much I travel and how unstable it is, there is no fucking way. You need six months of pure fucking detox to come off drugs, you can't do it in a month. Not with what I've got to cope with.'

I pitch in some more. 'Well, you know, you've got plenty of time. You're young but what you really need is a bit of stability to get off the gear. It's too much. A lot of people can handle habits, whatever, but the point of the matter is that it's no life long term. Really. That's my preach over. You know what I mean.'

I think she did. I hope she did. She deserves better. For all this talk about drugs, Carolyn is not quite sure about me. I am asking too many questions. She is puzzled and says so. Diego picks up on it and suddenly I find the tables have been turned. 'Mac, you know what, you always ask lot of questions about other people, but you never talk about yourself.'

Carolyn agrees, adding, 'That's the secret, because if I go down that road I'm going to find out things about myself that I don't want to know.'

I am clearly on difficult turf here. Diego continues the inquisition. 'He's a mysterious guy.' He gives me a considering look. 'You seem very obvious and very easy to understand [like] what you get is what you see.' He pauses and declares excitedly, 'I believe MAC is a SPY.'

I agree immediately, seeing no other course of action other than to fall on my sword. 'I'm full-time. I work for the Soviet Union [pause] and America.' We all laugh. I realize that, in all the time that I have spent with him, Diego is slowly developing insights into me – rather alarmingly accurate ones. I try to distract them from this line of inquiry by asking Carolyn about the pressures of being a model and trying to keep her weight down. It is magnificent to watch her at the table. She has not eaten properly for days and takes to the menu like a child, excited, giddy and irrepressible. 'Is it true you really got into a bit of coke to lose weight?'

'That's not the reason that I started, but then it became hard to give it up. My life became a binge.'

'But how do you control your weight?'

'Well, it's like, I stop doing drugs, because I'm doing too many. Then, when I first started to feel clean again after about two days, felt so weird, because my body's never clean of toxins, and I start eating, and I want to get healthy, but then I freak out about that. So I think the easiest way to lose weight is to do drugs again... Either that or you fucking go to the gym and work your arse off for three hours.'

I watch them and hope that I am watching a beautiful love story. I hope that when Diego is being gentle, caring and thoughtful, that he means it. I have no idea if he is being faithful – that is not my business. I haven't asked him about his Moonsinners points table because I don't want to know. As far as I'm aware Carolyn does not know about Diego's past. It would be soothing and maybe naive to believe him when he says he is going to be good for her. It is perhaps an indulgence for me to believe that Diego can finally leave his PR work behind and develop his photography career (if it exists). And a fantasy to expect the regime of stimulants and drugs to come to an end.

Theirs is a Sid-and-Nancy relationship. Carolyn is a sweet woman, but is lost in a haze of drugs and the whirlwind of fashion shows. Her frenetic lifestyle has trapped her in a pattern of behaviour which, as yet, she shows no sign of escaping. If drugs were taken out of the equation, Diego and Carolyn might even have a chance together. But while she's being encouraged to get off drugs by him, Diego, despite his advice, actively snorts cocaine with her. Carolyn wants to get off the gear; her booker at the Marilyn agency on Rue de la Paix in Paris also wants her to do this. Her booker is

Filipa da Cunha Reis and, like Diego, she is part of the problem. Filipa is a drug dealer and supplies Carolyn with drugs when the latter is in Paris. There is no suggestion that the agency is aware of Filipa's drug dealing. She keeps a stash in the office of the agency and charges inflated prices for the drugs she supplies. Carolyn recognizes the hypocrisy. Perhaps Filipa does too.

12th March 1999

Part of my team is here in Paris, supporting me on the ground, while the rest are back home progressing other stories. Our investigation into the Nigerian scam is still tiptoeing along and today, outside Manchester City Hall, another producer, Jonathan Jones, creates a substantial stepping stone on the way to entrapping the 'magic money' scammers.

He has hired two pretend models and one minor celebrity, Derek Hatton. The former deputy leader of Liverpool Council is quite a character and has agreed to help us out. He is now a broadcaster in Manchester and he is game for a laugh. Jonathan bought one bottle of champagne and printed a backdated metre-and-a-half-long cheque, purporting to represent winnings of £5.4 million. Retired policeman Peter Coles, the pretend lottery winner, poses and celebrates so enthusiastically that a large crowd gathers to celebrate with him. Our team photographer is taking the snaps. We haven't yet got the newspaper on board to do a mock-up front cover for us, but we should do shortly. People start hooting from cars and passers-by offer their congratulations. One smart onlooker inquires why the cheque is dated two years previously. It is explained by Jonathan that the winner had failed to claim his winnings until five days before the two-year deadline. The inquisitor is satisfied with this, although in fact there is a one-year deadline to claim all lottery winnings. The cheque is backdated for the purposes of the newspaper clipping only. It is supposed to fool the Nigerian 419ers and not the on-lookers.

Nonetheless, the ruse is working and should make a suitable photograph to further entice the fraudsters into our web. When Solomon comes back from Nigeria, a whole panoply of clues and newspaper clippings, photographs and props will await him to convince him that my story is genuine and that I really do have a lottery winner to serve up as a mark.

13th March 1999

After much negotiation, Gérald and I get to sit down for lunch at his favourite restaurant on Rue de Cherche Midi. I am a different person with Gérald today. I am confident enough to extract a laugh, sharp enough to discuss high corporate finance and open enough to let him know about my family's huge wealth in the oil business (invented). This is the Mac he knows – and more. He can fill in the blanks on who I am and why I dash in and out of his world with no apparent agenda other than good company. As a result, he is more honest and intimate than ever. We have moved on. The discussion starts more or less with hookers and we review the events at Williams the other night.

DONAL: 'You never told me what happened after Williams. I can't believe that we go to – what you call a whorehouse – and I get a headache. I had a very bad headache.'

GÉRALD: 'No, we brought back a Romanian with big lips, long hair – we brought back two or three of them, I forget... mine stayed there until breakfast.'
[He goes on to recommend an establishment in Miami: he says that she has a catalogue of all the prostitutes for one's perusal.]

DONAL: [Flippantly] 'It's like a model agency!'

GÉRALD: 'Same.'

He told me in Milan that he needs sex every day. I asked him what if he doesn't get it there and he said, 'That will never happen.' Though, he said, jokingly, he gets his period once a month. But today we cannot escape from sex, even when Gérald orders his starter. I ask him what he is having and he replies, 'I am having little pieces of octopussy,' smiling at the double entendre.

Gérald Marie is an unusual businessman with some unusual management techniques, which include rolling joints for his Elite staff. '...You move yourself to them – you have to – because it is not a very easy job that they do, they need support... it is really a family management... But in tough moments [brings his hands together quickly] – whoosh – they all get together, like this, and you cannot move them. It is, like, when they work in Fashion Week, we all work very hard, they all come to my room at any time, except from 9.30 to one o'clock in the morning, I cook.'

DONAL: 'You cook?'

GÉRALD: 'I cook, whatever. They come, they sit, I serve them, I roll them a joint and then they go back to work. But eventually they come back, for a coffee or a cognac, whatever. And we function that way.'

Interspersing this conversation is the long, lingering looks he gives to every attractive woman who passes by, to whom he purses his lips in admiration. No subject is sacrosanct, but there is a level of intense concentration when he discusses finance and his business. I ask him has he ever considered going to the market with his company.

GÉRALD: 'Yeah, but I think... we got everything ready to go on the market... but I don't really know if that's the key... And then I make a lot of money, but then I am paralysed... I don't know if this way to digest the system will be possible again if I am on the market because then you have to clear everything. If I have an employee that really works like an asshole that month [this is meant in a positive way – 'works his arse off' – something got lost in the translation], I would say, "Listen, you really deserve lots," and if I want to give him a couple of thousand bucks...'

DONAL: 'Lift up.'

GÉRALD: 'What can I do? What am I going to do? Nothing, I can't, and it's sad.'

At the moment he pays some of his staff in cash, but if he were to float ['on the stock market'] the company would come under more scrutiny and that would not be possible.

Business is business for Gérald and fun is fun and sometimes you can mix the two.

He invites me to the Elite model contest in September, where they have one big party. 'You have to see one thing we are doing in Nice, if you are in Nice in September. It's the contest, Elite Model Contest. This is something else – sixty-four kids in three weeks, on the same spot, real sunny and stuff like that, don't ask...'

DONAL: [Alluding to the women] 'It must be the most fantastic...'

GÉRALD: 'But me, I can't touch. If I touch one, the press will kill me. Finish. So that is why I go to... Williams, sometimes, and fuck around... Prostitutes are easier sometimes. But... Of course, sometime you can be photographing and you have something special, and if she talks [tells] you that, and she feels also similar, then of course you aren't going to [be] a monk and say, "I don't, I don't" – it's like a baker who doesn't eat the cake.'

Gérald is tempted, but does not succumb. He tells me an extraordinary story about a deal that was offered to him as the head of a model agency. An Arab man came in to him, offering him cash to buy some girls. Even Gérald was shocked. So am I and I'm just listening to the story.

'One day one guy came – the secretary of a king, I don't know, I forgot where – came with a suitcase – not an attaché case – with the money in cash and [put it] on my desk.' The man had offered Gérald money for models staying at an Elite residency in Paris. He thought that they were for sale. 'Sorry, no way,' Gérald said. 'Can you imagine the drama of the parents who gave you the kids, your daughter, she's sixteen years old and all of a sudden you sell all those kids to some Arabs?' This is the fashion world.

Gérald has warmed to me and before the day is out he invites me back to his house for a spliff. I say that I'll ring him later. He drops me off after we visit a tailor, where he is being measured up for some new shirts. I bid him farewell until the next time, but I don't think I will see him again. This is nearly the end of my journey in fashion. I still can't really understand why this man has taken me into his inner circle. No doubt he will be asking the same questions when my investigations are made public.

15th March 1999

I return to London. It's that old familiar route to Charles de Gaulle airport again. All the elements are finally coming together for this investigation and it's nearly wrapped up now. My mantra – 'We're in good shape' – is not just a morale-booster for the team or to placate Alex – it's the truth.

26th March 1999

It's time to add meat to the bones of the fraud investigation. This reverse scam has to be more sophisticated than any manoeuvres and tricks that the 'magic money' scammers try on any of their marks. Outwitting people is their business and now we have to beat them at their own game. To that end, producer Jonathan Jones and I go to *The News and Star* newspaper offices in Carlisle to mock up a front page. The editor offers to support our investigation and indeed knows Peter Coles from his policing days. The page declares our invented lottery winner as £5.4 million the richer. The dummy front page features the photo-shoot we arranged earlier in the month with Peter, our bogus lottery winner, where he was seen celebrating his winnings with champagne and displaying his winner's cheque. We figure that a final strand of evidence like this will encourage our friends to take our bait when they return from Nigeria. We are fishing. They are fishing. Who is going to catch whom?

(I have no idea what Solomon is doing today in Nigeria, but he will undoubtedly be aware that police chiefs from thirty countries are meeting there to discuss how best to end the 419 fraud that is bringing disgrace to Nigeria and causing untold economic damage across the globe. The fraud is being described as 'one of the most notorious economic crimes prevalent in the world today'. These high-level investigations may be making him more cautious.)

29th March 1999

Manchester Police have a court hearing 'in camera' (a private hearing) this morning to try and get hold of our footage covering the Manchester–Millwall match (at which one of the team was spotted with a video camera getting into my Mercedes, which was then traced back to the BBC). We are trying to get a deal to delay the handing over of the material for three weeks. We want to work with them, but they are nervous of us. There is a trust by-pass here and it is entirely understandable. Whatever happens, we will co-operate fully with police investigations into the riots there, but I am not sure that they believe us. Alex is phoning me with updates on an hourly basis.

2nd April 1999

An agreement was reached at the door of court yesterday, which was ratified by the judge in chambers. It was agreed that the police could view the material, with the caveat that they could do so only in the Manchester offices of the BBC. This was done to protect the team from any unfortunate leaks that might occur if the copies of our footage were distributed more widely. They agreed to give us twenty-four hours' notice if they were going to arrest anyone seen on the tapes, which would mean that defence solicitors would have access to the tapes and therefore so would their clients. This would have safety implications for anyone left operating in the field. This period of notice would give us time to pull out of the field and end the undercover investigation if it were unsafe to continue. The police also agreed not to reveal our investigation to anyone outside a select few. It is a relief that this has been sorted out.

Seven months ago I moved into Chelsea Close. Now my job is nearly done, it's time to move out. Ironically the man who is helping me move out is Jason, who was the very reason for me moving in initially. I'd come here to get close to him and hauled a sofa past him to get his attention. Now he is struggling to manoeuvre the self-same sofa back down three flights of stairs. Huffing and puffing, his cheeks flared and straining, Jason is here because he is my friend.

He might also be here because he wants a job. Jason's expertise is violence and mine, allegedly, is crime. Judging from the trappings of wealth Paul and I dazzle him with, it certainly looks as if crime pays. Such is the trust he now holds me in that he is offering the services of another mate of his, a fellow Head-hunter, to help us on a bogus cannabis run that is supposed to take place at the end of the season. It's no coincidence that this is the end of my tenure as a hooligan. The drug story and possible work deriving from it is aimed to protect us in the field until the end of the season. By the time Jason actually comes looking for work, the season will be over and so will our friendship.

6th April 1999

I am worried about the Nigerian fraudsters. I have not heard from them.

Today, US Secret Service agents arrested a major figure in the Nigerian 419 scam at his home in Hollywood, California. The US attorney's office has issued a statement saying that the suspect is linked to other suspects in a vast international criminal network of Nigerian frauds and scams. It occurs to me that perhaps this could be one of the reasons why Solomon is choosing to spend more time than usual in the safety of Lagos.

9th April 1999

In a photography studio somewhere in London I am sipping coffee. Today is all play. I turn the mobile off. We are photographing the front cover of this book. This building was once used to manufacture mannequins. Apparently, a male model came in to be photographed and said that he had been here before in order to be used as a mould for a mannequin. So they really do live!

13th April 1999

I phone The Penguin (Jason) to try and make contact and to thank him for the moving-out charade. In truth, I was moving out and he was a help and I tell him so. He is dealing with a couple of car pickups today, desperately trying to get together the £600 or so to pay for his season ticket. We were going to meet up, but he's distracted and cannot commit himself.

14th April 1999

I dreamed last night that I was driving along and I ran out of petrol. It doesn't take much to figure that one out. I've had one or two days off in the past few months and the strain is taking its toll. Got to hold it together. I am not consciously worrying about failure, but I am concerned about the tiredness.

Jason phones and we agree to meet in two days' time. I will debrief him comprehensively – set him up in a place where I can get clean sound and see what plans he has for Leicester. He has already said that he was 'up for it with Leicester on Sunday 2p.m.'. Don't know what that means yet.

Later, I take the familiar road to the care home. I take my time because it is a lunchtime appointment with the head of the home. I have come to talk about doing some more shifts. I have been on the phone to the home and they said that I could come and have a chat about other work if it became available, although my original post has been filled. I have told them that my crisis is over and that I am available for part-time work. They were accommodating on the phone and we are having a chat about it today. Some of the patients are outside the building when I walk up to it. They greet me and hug me. 'When are you coming back, Mike?' I say I don't know, but hopefully soon. They are warm. I have missed their company. I have not forgotten that they were my family over Christmas. I will never forget that.

The head of the home welcomes me and we discuss my doing further work. I say I can work Sundays and Mondays and she says that she'll have to run it by one of the directors. I suspect it won't be too much of a problem. She has it in mind for me to care for one particular patient at weekends and she says I should call in a couple of weeks' time.

16th April 1999

Jason is busy and we don't manage to meet. He is still up for going to the game. I am to phone him tomorrow.

I move into the safe house today, so concerned is the BBC about my security and any threats. It *is* secure and it *is* comfortable, but it is not a home. After the series and the publication of these investigations I will try to find one of those again. I have had to put my own house on the market because it is too close to the perimeters of the football investigation. I never thought that my job would impact so much on my own personal life. I don't regret it. I accept it as a price that has to be paid for this type of work.

17th April 1999

We don't want Jason to participate in violence. We have never filmed him being violent and we don't need to. We've heard him talking about it and we've witnessed the aftermath in Leicester. What we do need to witness is the organization. That has never been observed at close quarters before and it's at the heart of our investigations. Today, I am keen to meet Jason and ask him not to get into any trouble at the match tomorrow. I am going to say that if he wants to do any business with me (meaning the bogus drug-running) he should stay off the Old Bill's agenda.

I phone Jay but again he can't meet up. I wonder if anything is wrong. We decide to talk in the morning. I've been having strange dreams and not sleeping very well. Tonight I go out for a few beers.

18th April 1999

Ah, that must be a hangover. Or else there is a fridge on my head. I'll see how the crown feels later, before I call in the surgeons.

The plan is to go to the Chelsea vs Leicester game. The arrangement was to phone Jason. Thank God his phone is switched off. I go to the game with Paul and we practise our conversations about Chelsea on a couple of ordinary fans. It is preparation for any comprehensive scrutiny that we might be under if we go abroad with the Head-hunters again.

Some of them are lifelong supporters. I hold my own and they seem surprised at my knowledge. Most fans don't study their passion; it seeps in. There was no crash-course or Football Association seminar on 'How to be a Chelsea Fan'. I had to do some home study and I'm glad that I did. This has allowed Paul and me to operate safely in the field. It might do so again in Majorca, where Chelsea are playing next week in what might be their final game in Europe this season. I hope it is. Even football hooligans need a rest.

Jason's phone is still off.

19th April 1999

Jason is not going to Majorca: he can't afford it. I can hear sighs of relief in Spain as he speaks.

21st April 1999

Fly to Majorca. On the plane are BBC commentators John Motson, Ray Stubbs and Trevor Brooking. They have no idea that their other BBC colleagues, the ones dressed like football hooligans, are here to cover the match from an altogether different perspective.

22nd April 1999

There is the threat of violence on the terraces. There is the tremor of anticipation around the stadium. There is anger and distress in the air. Fans whisper in my ear that 'It's going to kick off, definitely, man'. But it doesn't. This rumble of football thugs has no leadership and, despite provocation and sporadic forays by the police into the crowd, there is no major trouble. It is obviously expected – the game sees the biggest police presence in the history of the island – but although all the elements for violence were there, the organization wasn't. The Head-hunters had promised violence, but they didn't travel. Football violence doesn't happen by serendipity or by chance. It is orchestrated.

23rd April 1999

There are some hooligans around, but we do not meet them. In 80-degree temperatures Pip wants Paul and I to go looking for them, wearing secret cameras with coats on to hide them. Roasted and toasted in three layers of clothes and wearing shades and a hat, I look like I'm dressed for a polar expedition. It's hilarious. Pip must have thought it was Copenhagen all over again. I have hardly left the hotel when the ridicule starts. 'Ain't you seen the weather forecast, mate?' Paul and I retreat – nay, race – to the hotel and divest ourselves of our extraneous clothing and most of the covert equipment, leaving only the mini disc for sound. There are familiar faces here, but the hard-core leadership isn't present.

24th April 1999

I try to phone Jason to talk football, but he is not answering. I do some pieces to camera and then enjoy the sun.

25th April 1999

Homeward bound. Jason is a bit elusive on the phone, but I finally get him just before my plane departs for London. The usual pleasantries are exchanged. He has just finished playing football, which he won 8–1. He says he had a dog's breakfast of a game. Every time I speak to him I try to weigh up every hesitation, gap and cadence to ascertain if his mood towards me has changed. I worry constantly that he may be concerned I'm not who I say I am. But today there is no problem. Jason is warm. I don't need to fret. Not today, anyway.

26th April 1999

Jill Dando has been killed. A single gunshot to the head. I am in my car when I hear the news. I park up near a church in Twickenham, the same one where Dermot Morgan's (Father Ted's) memorial service was held. I say a brief prayer. It's the first time, other than for baptisms and weddings, that I've ventured into a church in years.

A memorial is set up at the BBC offices in White City and people stand and stare at it in distress. I am numb with shock. It's a terse and terrible reminder that this is only television and no fame or stardom is worth this madness. There is some debate over whether there should have been a news flash because of her death. Either way, I just feel for her family.

Our concerns regarding the PACE (Police and Criminal Evidence Act) order – the court order that allowed the Manchester Police to view our footage of the Millwall–Manchester City fixture – were confirmed today when we got a call from a newspaper journalist working on a sports desk asking about the footage from the Manchester–Millwall match. The journalist was doing some research on the violence at the match and was given information about the confidential PACE order. It means someone has leaked the information, which, quite apart from being in contempt of the court order, is annoying and, what's more, foolhardy. We are still in the field and it is too dangerous to allow such sensitive information into the public domain in case it falls into the wrong hands. Luckily the sports editor knows Pip and he cordially agrees to spike the story on safety grounds.

We are busy trying to find out the source of the leak – there are only a tiny number of people who know as the PACE order was held in camera, precisely because of the potential risks to us. Whether we should go back to court and complain or hope it just dies away is a hard one to call. We decide not to press too many buttons, but will continue to monitor developments.

Yet more bad news: Rex, the father of a close friend of mine, has been ill for some time. I have been in contact with him since Christmas and he has given me great support. He is a former Fleet Street journalist and at seventy-eight can still write me off the page. I hope he gets better.

27th April 1999

A couple of friends call me, worried about my safety. No need to worry, I say. I am in a safe house. The real danger occurs when I come out of the field and reveal myself to my protagonists. There have been no more death threats, but it does set you thinking. Having said that, I try not to dwell on it.

Pip has phoned the head of the Football Intelligence Unit, one of the parties present when our case was heard in chambers. He assures us that the leak did not come from his organization. He agrees to remind the police officers involved that it is contempt of court to reveal the information outside agreed channels.

As I sip my coffee today, I read a headline in the *Daily Mail* that brings back the two months I spent in a crack den in Wembley in April and May 1997 to expose an immigration scam: 'Mercy For Drug Girl in Bogus Bride Scam'. The story says that a former drug addict who went through several bogus marriage ceremonies to fund her 'voracious' crack cocaine habit was freed yesterday. 'Their activities came to the attentions of an investigative journalist who befriended them and then secretly filmed them.' The judge agreed with the defence summation that to send the girl to jail would only hamper her drug rehabilitation. He is quoted as saying, 'I suspect that, had it not been for the vigour and determination of your mother and father in leading you to this point, twelve months free of drugs, I have little doubt you would be going to prison and facing other charges, if indeed you were alive to do so.'

I am pleased that she did not go to jail. She was a victim of her habit and that was the seed for her criminality. I am glad to see justice take a sensible course.

30th April 1999

The BBC is still in mourning. Jill Dando's murder has scared me more than any death threat I have ever received. The bubble has burst. Now other BBC journalists have received warnings and, whether they're genuine or not, they're being treated as such and security has been stepped up. That protective envelope that sets the BBC apart and gives its presenters distance from those who would want to do them harm has been destroyed. They are now accessible and demonstrably so. It has set a precedent. May Jill Dando rest in peace.

Jason is keen to get together again. I say we should talk next week or meet at the game on Saturday. He is happy to co-operate as he's still sniffing after our bogus drugs deal. We're pleased, too, because it gives us the chance to debrief him fully about his right-wing links – he has changed his mobile number now because of the intense spotlight on the far right after the two recent bombs in Brixton and Brick Lane. There is no mention of the bombs in our conversation this afternoon.

A few hours later another bomb goes off in the gay quarter on Old Compton Street in London. It's thought to be another attack by the far right. Blacks, Asians, gays: Jason hates them all. I have seen his prejudices in full and brutal Technicolor over the past nine months. He is not involved, but he shares the prejudices.

1st May 1999

My 'mate' Andy 'Nightmare' Frain is in the papers. The *Guardian* headline reads, 'Racist Soccer Thug Jailed'. The story continues: 'A football hooligan, linked to the racist group, Combat 18, was yesterday jailed for 14 months and banned from soccer matches for five years by a judge at Reading Crown Court. Andrew Frain, 35, a former Grand Hawk in the Ku Klux Klan, attacked a mounted police officer at a match between Oxford United and Reading.'

I phone Danny, the Reading hooligan who runs (fights) with Chelsea, and ask him about Nightmare. Danny says he'll be out in six weeks because of the time he's already spent on remand. I ask after Danny and he tells me he's up in court himself on 21st May. I say I might be able to drive him. In the meantime, he's going to send Andy my regards when he visits him in prison. I remember the terror Paul and I felt when Nightmare arrived unannounced for the trip to Leicester and shudder. It's a relief to see him locked away. I just wish that he could stay away, off the streets, because they certainly are safer with him inside. So am I.

3rd May 1999

I have not spoken of my nails recently. I no longer carry my once constant companion Stop 'n' Grow in my pocket. Unfortunately, there has been no progress and no change. Once a biter, always one. I think it's genetic, myself. Other than that, coffee remains my faithful addiction – I consume up to fifteen cups a day. Some days it is very good for me and some days very bad, depending on the latest research published in the small columns of the broadsheet newspapers that I read for my daily diet of health-scare stories.

4th May 1999

Rex passed away during the night. He helped me with this diary, giving me advice. 'Save a laugh for every page, it's easier on the reader,' he always said. We talked on the phone in the months before he was taken ill and he told me the way to get through the work was to treat it as just one block upon another. Rex had death threats as a journalist and we forged a strange affection for each other.

7th May 1999

A canary-yellow Porsche Boxster drives up to Solomon's London base in Wembley. It is an ordinary, unspectacular home, not too ostentatious – certainly not enough to attract unwanted attentions. The car is hired as a prop for the day. Solomon is impressed by material things and, even if he is still holed up in Nigeria, his friends, who are holding the fort there, will report back. My colleague hands over a copy of the newspaper front page declaring our invented lottery winner a millionaire five times over. Solomon's friends promise to fax the cutting over to Nigeria. With Solomon's appetite thus whetted, we anticipate a speedy return.

8th May 1999

We hear from Nigeria. Solomon is going to be back shortly. He is clearly hungry for a slice of the lottery pie. It's a relief to know that he is making arrangements to return. I wondered if I would ever see him again. I was afraid that I had scared him off or that his antennae had been too sharp for my ruse.

The first thing on Solomon's agenda will be an unveiling of his strategems to entrap Peter and his money. A trip to Ghana will be arranged and a fake ex-president's son conjured out of thin air. We are all ready to fly out to the frontline of this infamous international scam. Solomon has previously promised to provide armed security for Peter and his entourage – my team. We will be armed, too. With cameras. Hopefully, we will film this scam in action and frame the fraudsters the same way they've netted their marks: using their greed for bait. But to land a fish as big and canny as Solomon, nothing must go wrong... If they spot our cameras, what will happen? People who have tried to challenge the 419ers have not lived to tell the tale. This could be the most dangerous assignment of the year.

10th May 1999

'Round up all you know, there are two groups of Chelsea, thirty and forty strong...' The Tottenham mob is assembling. I am Chelsea and am standing just 10 metres away. I am definitely in the wrong place. It is the two teams' traditional end-of-season clash – for which read their supporters' organized end-of-season scrap. There is revenge to be extracted. Earlier this year, some of the

Chelsea were jailed after a clash with Spurs the previous season. The Tottenham fans committed a major sin. They 'turned' – that is, they gave evidence against their rivals to save their own necks. Something like that is not forgotten.

I enter the field today – my last day out as a Head-hunter – while Chelsea go to war. The match is completely superfluous; this is about getting even. But today I am feeling more vulnerable than usual. My two Head-hunter friends, Jason and Nightmare, are not around. I have been on tour with the Head-hunters, even been anointed as a new recruit, so I am confident that I will survive; nevertheless I am without patronage.

Jason – who is nursing a wicked hangover and is too ropy to attend – warned me about it earlier in the day. Even he told me to 'keep your head down'. Paul and I go to the appointed meeting place, a pub close to Highbury and Islington tube station. There are about forty Head-hunters in the pub. The atmosphere is terse and tense, with lots of gritting and grinding of teeth. Amphetamines and cocaine are being consumed by everyone in the toilet – it's so blatant that the door is ajar and there is a queue of ten fans waiting to get in for a snort. Some of the fans I recognize from Copenhagen and Leicester, but I don't know them that well and without Jason or Nightmare, who is banged up, I feel a little exposed. Paul looks at me and I look at him. He knows what I'm thinking.

I turn my camera on to get a shot of the crowd. (It transpires that the covert equipment broke down. I have sound but no pictures. It makes me feel like a wonky tube television. There's more static around me than your average million-volt pylon.) My body stays still and I move my head and take a puff from a cigarette. Judging from the glances coming from the group, I know that we're causing a disturbance. I have seen them before and they have seen me before, but a combination of police surveillance – the place outside is crawling with cops – and their own latent violent intent and drug-infused paranoia means that we are being regarded as suspicious. I am horribly aware of this. I sniff and squeeze my nostrils like a cocaine user would, then check my watch and deliberately blow smoke into my eye. My eyes are now bloodshot, giving me the appearance of a hardened substance abuser. There is a partial recovery, but the taint remains.

The word goes out and the pub empties. We follow the mob into the tube station, only to be overtaken by a troop of fifteen police officers who are carrying a camera to video the gang. We retreat to the shadows and they pass by without noticing. The train pulls in and we jump on with the hooligans and join them in their game of cat and mouse with the police. We all get off at the next stop but one and that is when we get separated from the Chelsea mob.

From that moment, I feel vulnerable. If you are not with them, then you are apart from them. If you are apart, then the game is over. We eventually get to the Park Lane end of the Tottenham ground, and the police presence is entrenched. It is then that I hear, unusually for the football hooliganism world, a black man lead the Spurs troop into action against the Chelsea mob we have become lost from. (It dawns on me that the Chelsea mob perhaps thought that I was not the police but a Spurs fan, which is much worse in their eyes.)

The police are close by and so it seems are the Chels. I am rigged up and still believe that the equipment is working. Suddenly, a line of police sweep across the road and I am caught in a flurry of fans. Spurs fans. They are spewing vitriol at the blue Chelsea supporters nearby. 'Is he Chelsea? Let me at 'im,' one says, fully intent on thrashing a Chelsea fan who is standing a couple of metres from me. A policeman starts to intervene.

'Behave, mate, or I'll nick you.'

'But I ain't done anything, mate,' the fan shouts back.

'I'll make it up,' retorts the cop. Now I am standing shoulder-to-shoulder with people who would dearly love to kick and tear and headbutt me, just because I follow another team. It's alarmingly ludicrous. They have not identified me or Paul as Chelsea yet. The longer I investigate football, the more I wonder why these people care so much to fight for their club. I still haven't got an answer. I tell myself it's best not to intellectualize it and just get out of there. Sneaking off to the side of the road, Paul and I beat a hasty retreat from the home fans.

The game has kicked off late because of the problems of getting the Chelsea fans safely to the match. I see they are searching people entering the ground and have to go off to an empty parking lot where I de-rig myself of my covert equipment and all its internal microphones, circuitry and wiring – and the high levels of microwaves. There is so much to wear in order to be a one-man covert film crew that it's not a matter of feeling positive or negative in the field, it's a matter of being electrically charged. Some day I will internally combust.

Having removed my camera rig and given it to Pip, who was behind me while I was following the Chelsea mob, I put my clothes back on and return to the ground. A man is selling two tickets for the Chelsea end. I buy them and Paul and I go in. I am searched and padded down. The game is already in full flow and Chelsea are one up. Taking my seat, I realize that the two people who were looking at me in the pub are sitting above me. To the right is Stuart Glass, who was acquitted in the Own Goal trial ten years ago. I last saw him on video, snorting cocaine at the World Cup. The police have spotted him, too. He is surrounded by his acolytes. I catch his eye. That is a mistake. I stare in front and pretend to take no notice of him, but he continues to stare in my direction. Paul glances over at me. His look says the game is up. Stuart is still staring. Does he think we are Old Bill or Spurs? He has never seen me with Jasøn or Nightmare, so he doesn't know my invented history. As far as Stuart Glass is concerned, I do not belong. He will freeze me out.

At half-time the police decide not to intervene to get the Headhunters out of the ground. They are probably worried that it may inflame an already hostile atmosphere. Although they have separated the two sets of supporters, even the police can't stop the venom echoing across the terraces: 'I've got a foreskin, haven't you?'

The game is over and the fans filter out. There are fifty police surrounding the Chelsea mob. I am back in a dark alleyway trying to re-rig my covert equipment retrieved from Mark R., who is helping out Pip tonight. There is a technical problem again with the kit, a combination of robust handling and sensitive equipment. At this stage I am 300 metres adrift of the gang. I have to catch up. I run and run. I am out of breath with the equipment on my back and eventually make contact at the back of the group. A policeman tries to stop me joining up with my brethren.

'I'm Chelsea, I'm Chelsea, mate,' I plead. I join up, but soon meet resistance. It is one of the guys from the pub. He was part of the suspicious brood. He doesn't trust me and tells me so.

'You're a bit nervous,' he says. I ignore him. 'You're sweating a bit,' he says again. He isn't to know that I am sweating because I had to run up to catch him, to film him. I presume he thinks I am either police or Spurs.

'What's your problem, mate?' I respond firmly.

'It's no surprise that you're sweating mate, is it?'

The troop of around fifty Chelsea is about to be herded into the tube station. Together. I could drag out my Jason line and my other connections, but that could mean blowing Jason out for good. If I just resign now, Jason might still be a viable option – for a few days more, anyway. I look at this small, dumpy, bald, venomous individual and I know that he knows that I am not one of them. I remember the look Stuart Glass gave me with its promise of something more menacing. I cannot go in with them. Not without risking my safety. The game is up.

I walk away. It took me nearly a year to get there and just a few seconds to leave it behind. I am no longer a Head-hunter. It's over. I cross to the other side of the road and meet up with Paul. He looks at me. We shake hands, a firm handshake, then we hug. We are safe.

23rd May 1999

I have not heard from Nigeria or from Solomon. He promised to call to alert me to his return, but has not. He has not returned and he has not called. This may be the end of the investigation. It is disappointing because government departments have been put on alert after several civil servants reported scam attempts on Whitehall offices. This scam is always at work – it is truly all-pervasive – but if Solomon doesn't call there can be no progress in the investigation. He may remain the illusive and unfortunately successful con man that he is.

12th June 1999

Gérald invites me to take behind-the-scenes photographs of the Moscow heat of the Elite Model Look Competition, a contest for potential young models spanning fifty-seven countries, with over 350,000 entries. The invite comes out of the blue. In fact out of the blue sea off the coast in Spain. I am here in Ibiza, also at Gérald's invitation. He is generous with invites to his friends and he counts me as one now. I thought it was a boys' weekend, but he has his girlfriend here, so I don't record any pictures. This is a private holiday – too private for me. As soon as I arrive, I try to arrange my escape. I fly into the Spanish resort and spend three hours in Gérald's company and buy him lunch before asking him to drop me off at the airport, apparently to head off on a late photoshoot call in London. Of my jetsetting travel arrangements, he says: 'Typical Mac – he flies in just for lunch.' The invite to Moscow resonates with 'sexual connotations'. I promise to be there.

7th July 1999

I had given up on the fraud investigation but, today, Solomon and I talk on the phone. He is in Nigeria and I am in London. He is concerned to tell me that the business is still on – that he is still interested in helping me to separate our invented lottery winner, Peter, from his easily earned cash. The cherry picker is still open for business. 'Don't let him spend all the money, please,' he pleads. He still stutters and it is more pronounced on the phone. Nonetheless, there is an arrogance and determination resonating down the line. I am firm with him, interested but not grovelling, and I'm focused and alert – alert to the fortune that apparently awaits Solomon and me, if we can pull this joint enterprise off together. He needs to trust me and I have to be seen and heard sizing Solomon up, too – just as I would if this were a real scam and not a reverse scam: to dupe the con men and sting the stingers.

He has a story prepared to fill in the gaps for my lottery winner. Arrangements are made to further the scam in the first week of August in either Amsterdam or London. Then we will go to West Africa for the last and most dangerous chapter in the fraud investigation. We will go to their turf and be at their mercy as we try to reveal the mechanics of this malevolent scam. I now know more of their violence and their methods and I am tense at the prospect.

12th July 1999

The logistics of filming secretly in Russia are terrifying. Moscow and the rest of the country are rife with corruption, and nearly 500 businessmen have been killed in this year alone. It is a dangerous place and it is not made any safer with covert equipment strapped around one's body. We disguise our covert cameras as overt equipment in order to get through customs. It is a victory just to get through here. They look very carefully at my ten-year-old passport, search my bags and let me through. Colin and Paul, who have travelled with me, are sweating until I manage to talk my way into the country as a computer professional . The first hurdle is over. Now I have to spend time with Gérald and some of his business colleagues from Elite – but it's forty degrees outside and he will have bodyguards. I will have to be very careful. Out here there is no safety net.

13th July 1999

Paul and Colin, in a delicate engineering feat, assemble the secret cameras and undercover kit. I observe nervously until the last camera is fully crafted and ready to go. I return to my hotel, the Metropol, one of the finest hotels in Moscow and the same hotel that Gérald will be staying at when he arrives tomorrow.

I take a walk in Red Square and drop into a small Russian orthodox church off the main square, and pause to absorb the beautiful icons on the walls and the poverty of many of the Russians at prayer. It's hard to make any comparisons between the opulence of the hotel and the hungry beggars who line the streets here. Tomorrow Gérald and his fashion circus arrive to judge the hundreds of young hopefuls who are investing their dreams in the 1999 Elite Model Look Competition.

14th July 1999

The competition is being hosted by a local agent for Elite, a company called Red Star Models. I see it advertised on television. This is an expensive trip and it's probably the last time I'll meet Gérald Marie. The next few days are crucial to the investigation. Colin makes that perfectly clear to me. I am nervous about my safety and desperate not to disappoint Colin and the rest of the team. They are counting on me.

Gérald appears in the late afternoon and we arrange to meet in a casino restaurant just outside the centre of the city. I arrive in a taxi and am confronted by men wearing bulletproof vests and carrying guns. I look a bit puffed up because of the cameras and because I am a little heavy at nearly fifteen stone – I'll have to go on a diet. Gérald looks at me and welcomes me with open arms to the table.

'My God, they take their security seriously here', I say to him.

'Yeah, because of the gambling. They have Kalashnikovs everywhere,' Gérald explains, eyes dancing.

'Oh, my God. My first night in Moscow and here we are. There are Kalashnikovs everywhere', I say jokingly, but the subtext of my voice speaks loudly of fear; at least to those who know me well.

The night ends in a brothel called Nightflight. Gérald is so keen to put me at ease that he chooses a girl for me to take back to the hotel. Paul and Colin are also keeping their distance. I meet them and tell them my dilemma.

'He's got me a prostitute. What do I do?' We decide that I should make an early exit with the girl (she's about twenty-four) lest Gérald wants to share her with me in his room. I leave and just outside the club a soldier stops me and the prostitute. I have no papers and the soldier forces me to pay a $100 bribe to prevent him taking me to the police station. I don't want to go there wearing covert kit, so I hand over the money. I get into the woman's car as she says she'll drive me to the hotel.

I phone Colin and put on my mini-disc to record the conversation I have with her in case Gérald later accuses me of the same conduct he is guilty of. I also keep the phone line open to Colin and explain to him that I am going to accept the lift to the hotel and then say that I don't want to do any business. I pay her $300 and say that I have diabetes and can't make love. I apologize and ask her not to go back to my friends (Gérald *et al*) because I don't want them to know about my problem. She offers to help me, but I decline and that's how I make my excuses and leave.

15th July 1999

The dining area in the Metropol is in a huge cavernous room that harks back to a former gilded and prosperous era. I join Gérald Marie and the president of the Elite Model Look Competition, Xavier Moreau for breakfast. Xavier tells Gérald that there were nearly 1000 girls there yesterday, but they have been shortlisted today for provisional judging. Gérald, in his own inimitable manner, smiles and calls it 'a stadium of pussy'.

We are picked up in a black Lincoln and taken to the building where they are holding the competition. The driver provided for Gérald is also a bodyguard and looks after everyone in Gérald's party. For the moment that includes me. There are girls queuing up the street. Inside Gérald tells me that the BBC (Colin) asked for permission to film, but he refused them because he doesn't like them. He says that they are only trouble. I could only agree with him. Part of the problem is that Moscow newspapers are asking the question whether Red Star is a model agency or whether it's an escort agency. Both Red Star and Gérald are sensitive to the publicity fallout.

I am called up to the top table where the judging panel (Gérald et al) sit. I take pictures for Gérald as requested and I improvize. Sometimes there is film in the camera and sometimes there isn't. As the young girls parade up and down, Xavier keeps the conversation base, discussing the merits and prices of prostitutes at the club last night. It is a long day and we return to the hotel. Gérald crashes out, exhausted.

I meet Xavier and another Elite executive, Olivier Daube, director of recruitment and model placement. Olivier is based in New York and works with Daniele, the ex-PR and Elite live-in chaperon who I first met in Milan last December.

At Xavier's suggestion, we three go to the brothel for dinner. There, Xavier, who runs the world's biggest model contest – the Elite Model Look Competition, shares a little of his background with me and Olivier, his colleague. He says of Africa, 'It would be a great country if they were all white.'

'...So sad...I don't like black girls,' Xavier tells me.

I heard this racist line before in Gérald's room in Milan, when his business partner in Paris called the black footballers 'niggers'.

Having inquired about my fashion tee-shirt, which carried my covert camera, he talks about corporate hospitality in fashion. He tells me of the time he arrived in one country to be picked up in a limousine with a prostitute inside for his delectation.

'You have a limousine waiting for me, American limousine, a stretch, and a girl called Lolita. A blonde girl.' He says she was seventeen years of age. 'With a short little dress…like a baby doll. No panties. The chauffeur closed the partition, so I start to kiss… after that she took off the dress and jumped on me.'

Xavier is in his late fifties, bald and hugely overweight. He was given a blow job by the girl. This is not intimate conversation between close friends – this is bar room chat among fashion insiders. I pretend to enjoy his conversational titbits.

Olivier joins in, despite having only met me for the first time yesterday. He tells me that he was worried after he went to bed with a sixteen-year-old model. 'Once, you find a girl and go to your place and she's with her mum and her agent. She's talking to you and you fly in a plane. After a few hours' talking to her, she puts her head on your shoulder and at the airport she takes your hand. You take her home and you fuck her. And she's only sixteen.'

I say, 'That's fashion, you know,' trying to be as neutral as possible.

Olivier continues, 'That's fantastic but, at the same time, once you fucked her, you don't know what situation you are in. It happened to me, one case like that. I talked to the mum, I talked to the agent, I talked to the girl and fucked for a week like she never knew what happened to her. I was so horny and she was happy to get it.' Olivier is relishing the memory with gesticulation.

Later, Olivier sets the business in perspective, appropriately enough in a brothel.

'It's the same thing with a hooker that with a contestant…'

I check what I've heard. 'The contestants are the same as hookers?'

He replies unequivocally: 'Oh yeah, and we are pimps. You know that.'

I pay for the meal. They may regret my hospitality. Xavier goes off with a prostitute to the hotel while Olivier tries to persuade me to share a girl with him and asks some of the girls if they'll take two men at once. Before it gets out of hand, I feign a diabetic attack again and ask to be taken back to the hotel. He returns to the hotel with me. He walks me to my room to ensure that I'm all right. I appreciate the concern and we part – the excuses made and the night over.

16th July 1999

Today is the final of the competition. In the morning Gérald and I go shopping for tourist trinkets. We gather at the Radisson Hotel for the final of the Moscow heat of the Elite Model Look Competition. Again, Red Star provides us with black limousines and bodyguards. I am a friend of Gérald's and his patronage affords me entry to the top circle. Everybody is dressed up sharply. Everybody except me. I am dressed up in my photographer's jacket and it hides my covert camera gear very well. I take a picture of Gérald and the girls on stage. The room is full of photographers and video cameras. Colin has talked his way in too. The winners are selected and the party moves on inevitably to a strip joint called Dolls.

I am going into the club with Gérald. My body is laden down with covert cameras. It is the Moscow Mafia's favourite strip joint. For $100 a dancer will perform two erotic dances for you and for $2000 she will sleep with you, though only if she likes you – it's that kind of club. There are armed bodyguards at the entrance and airport-style metal detectors! The last owner was shot dead by a single round in the head by an assassin from a rooftop across the street. I have to go in – there is no alternative. There'll be one mess to sort out if they catch me. Here goes...

I bleep like a pinball machine. The owner greets Gérald and the Red Star boss. He greets me, though less effusively since the alarms have gone off. I gesture that I have photographic equipment that sets them off. Sweat drips down my back and I start to smoke, now at a rate of twenty an hour. Anything to keep busy.

Inside the club naked dancers perform around a pole on the centre stage. One dancer is provided to each of us as a treat by the owner. I pass on mine to Olivier. He now has two naked women caressing him. He watches and laughs, but he doesn't touch. Gérald is being entertained too. The conversation rarely moves from sex. Gérald once again invites me to the final of the Elite Model Look Competition in Nice in September. The invitation comes with a promise of fun – apparently with some of the models in the contest. It surprises me that he is prepared to mix his business with his pleasure and that he is prepared to offer the competition as a playboy's paradise for his friends. I probe him for evidential purposes.

'Nice, are we allowed to play with the girls?' I ask.

'I tell you when it's the moment or not,' Gérald says. 'Just give me guidance because I don't want to make any mistakes,' I insist.

Gérald fills me in on the details.

'In Nice I come with a big boat, which we will sleep on...in the Port...a few girls that I like... I will organize a dinner, a lunch...we sleep on the boat and we get off the boat to go and look at the girls and this and that...oh and you and you and you....I always have a couple of friends in there for girls...'

DONAL:	'There is no parents?'
GÉRALD:	'No, no.
DONAL:	'No parents on the boat, or chaperons.'
GÉRALD:	'We pay the chaperons.'
DONAL:	'We'll pay the chaperons, it's fine, to keep quiet.'
GÉRALD:	'The agency pays the chaperon. We go with the girls who like to go with us. We're not pushy. [To the girls] You wanna go with us?'
DONAL:	'With the girls in Nice, there'll be no comeback, will there?'
GÉRALD:	'Nothing.'
DONAL:	'Nothing.'

I feel relieved. Gérald has, by his own words, confirmed that the chaperon system is not to be trusted – not even that belonging to the biggest and best-known model agency in the world. Later, Olivier and I chat with Gérald.

'I know this man [Gérald] only from reputation. So when I joined the group [Elite] –'

Olivier is interrupted by Gérald, who calls it 'the sex group'. Olivier continues: 'You see those men are such womanizers but they still look at fresh blood like a very exciting thing. It's great.'

'It's normal,' says a smiling Gérald.

The night ends with Gérald chastizing Olivier, one of the Elite group directors, for incompetence because he was prevaricating over how much to offer a prostitute for sex in Nightflight. For the first time no excuses were needed because Gérald wanted to talk and we all then had a licence to go back to the hotel empty-handed.

17th July 1999

Gérald is leaving the hotel and is returning to Paris. I send him off. We agree to meet in Nice. The offer still stands then. He walks through the swinging doors. The black limousines pick up his party and my nightmare is over. Now there is time to exhale. I wonder what Gérald will think and say when he finds out exactly who I am?

6th September 1999

I talk to Gérald on the phone and the invitation to Nice still remains open. He is in his usual effusive mood.

'I never been eating so much pussy in a weekend. Pussy like strawberry pie.'

The plans are still in place for 'fun' at the Elite Model Look Competition.

'Sixty-four girls until the 11th and then, starting at twelve in the morning, we keep the fifteen best ones... Everybody leaves and just stay a few of us with only the fifteen. Aaahh...' He ends with gleeful anticipation.

EPILOGUE

My lives are winding down. My own life may take off, given the chance. It seems like a distant haze as I reflect on the road from the catwalks of Milan to the violence of Copenhagen, a journey that encompassed my lonely Christmas in care and my game of psychological chess with Solomon and my terrifying drive to Leicester with the Head-hunters. It is too much to take in at the moment. Even reading this diary, I can hardly believe where we've been and who we have met. It all seems unreal to me. While the words have remained constant on the page – the lives I looked at have moved on. For the moment this is where we are with our tandem lives and the in-tandem investigations. I have had to end the diary where I did to accommodate publisher's deadlines.

The fashion world remains pretty much as it was when I joined it over a year ago. The models still harbour childish dreams in an adult world. Many still falter at all the traditional pitfalls that fashion presents to newcomers. The PRs still compete in their sordid league, chaperons still fail to chaperon and Gérald Marie is still President of Elite Europe, the biggest model agency in the world. Diego and Carolyn have split up. He continues to be a 'part-time photographer' and full-time PR. She continues to model successfully. Meanwhile I continue to be a bad photographer.

The British heat of the Elite Model Look Competition took place in London in the middle of August. Xavier Moreau, who I had met in Moscow, was presiding. There was no talk from the podium of how he doesn't 'like black girls' or of the seventeen-year-old 'baby doll' prostitute called Lolita he enjoyed as corporate hospitality on another fashion business trip. The London leg was won by a fourteen-year-old white girl. Whatever her and the other winners' dreams and whatever their success, they might soon learn that fashion is very different from the inside looking out. From knowing nothing about fashion, I ended up knowing too much.

I found out that it is an ugly business about beautiful women but run almost entirely by men.

When I arrived in Nice, there was a boat in the bay at Gérald's disposal. The playboy's arena seemed all set up. I was preparing to reveal my identity to Gérald to prevent him from making any advances to the girls. The average age of the final selected group (by Elite's figures) was fifteen, and the age range varied from thirteen to seventeen; the winner was fourteen. Gérald's plan, to isolate a group of the girls, was intact until the night before the photoshoot on the boat, when he decided it was too risky and that too many people were watching. He said that he had to be careful because the Press and, particularly the 'British Press', would kill him. He pulled back because of media scrutiny and because the girls were sleeping two and three to a room and, if together, they would talk; it turned out that the shoot had to end the next afternoon – the boat became unavailable. He told me it would be easier when they were working in Milan or Paris. I was thankful for the girls' sake.

Gérald had all his team there, including his partner and senior director in Elite Model Fashion (the clothing end of the Elite empire), Roberto Caan, who was calling black footballers 'niggers' in Milan earlier this year. In Nice Roberto finished the fashion loop for me when he revealed how much he loved the Milanese PRs and how he invited some of Milan's most famous PRs to share his holiday villa in Ibiza during the summer. Roberto told me this while he was bemoaning the fact that he had run out of cocaine.

Later, on 10th September 1999, the drug supplier in the Marilyn Agency in Paris, Filipa da Cunha Reis, independently sold me a gram of cocaine for 800F in the agency office in much the same way as she sold it to Carolyn Park. The booker, with her wild nest of blonde hair and her gold necklace spelling out 'sexy' hanging from her neck, explained that she gave Carolyn the drugs as a means of monitoring her habit. It seemed to me that she also sold her the drugs as a means of making money.

Will anything change after this investigation? I don't know, but for the future I hope the explicit portrayal of the PR system in Milan will end PRs' reign for ever. It might be too much to ask for the industry to change dramatically, but the picture Gérald Marie draws of himself will encourage searching questions to be asked of him and the industry. This might well move the fashion world incrementally towards the real world. At the very least, I hope that our insider's guide will remind parents that sometimes bright lights shine too brightly.

Solomon invited me to his house in Wembley at the end of the summer. I showed him the newspaper clipping we mocked up. He looked convinced – I thought. The next day, as we made arrangements to meet his gang to move the scam on in Amsterdam, Solomon pulled out. He had all the props and clues but he didn't rely on research. He relied on intuition. That was his biggest weapon, and it worked well. Solomon said that his people were nervous. He didn't trust me. The deal was off. The con man put on the breaks. Nonetheless, Solomon had already revealed to us in his own words the *modus operandi*, although we haven't seen the scam operate on Peter. I can't help thinking, though, that Solomon the fraudster has won the battle of wits.

All is not lost. Having been rumbled by Solomon, we have moved onto another gang of 419 con men – and learning from our previous mistakes we are tiptoeing our way into their confidence. It is a delicate adventure and it's not over yet. It hasn't cost me anything to lose out to Solomon but how much has it cost others?

The care home investigation has been the most difficult. The evidence we have already will, I hope, make people stop and think about how we should best look after those who can't look after themselves. I have not been back to my hometown since the investigation into the care home started. But more than ever I am proud of the way it shares its town and community with the residents of the care home at the heart of the town. Other towns and other homes might yet learn lessons from it.

The investigation will shed more light on an industry already under scrutiny. There needs to be better training, higher wages and greater awareness of the difficulty of being a full-time carer. Whether our investigation succeeds in any of these remains to be seen.

I still have my Chelsea FC tattoo and football violence is still hitting the headlines. The first day of the new football season arrived and nothing changed. While Jason prepared to sit in his season-ticket seat at Stamford Bridge, the Millwall 'troops', who I travelled with earlier in the year, were organizing 'war' on Cardiff City through the internet. 'Get ready, Taffies, we are coming to wreck your country', the computer-literate hooligan promised. While that was in full flow, Bristol City fans were attacking some of the Reading and Chelsea fans on the Danger Gang's own turf.

Old scores are still settled up and down the country, long after the original sin has been forgotten. Last season, arrests for serious football violence doubled as hooligans such as Jason became more sophisticated. For all his sophistication, though, Jason is still a head-hunter and a second-hand tyre merchant. Andy 'Nightmare' Frain is out of jail and lying low. Danny is just back from holidays in Greece, hoping that he doesn't get an extended one at Her Majesty's pleasure.

Football hooliganism doesn't go away. It will never go away. I have tried to leave it behind but, until I get my tattoo removed, I know that I will still be stained by the vitriol, violence and rancid xenophobia of my fellow Head-hunters – my former friends. My friendship rested in their eyes only.

The police and the clubs are doing their best to eradicate and crush violence around 'the beautiful game'. But ultimately they might have to admit defeat in the fight against hooliganism. The stain runs so deep in our society that not even the exclusion of the trouble-makers has worked. It cannot succeed. Disaffected young men will always fight and have only to find a cause on which to pin their aggression. Football has been and will remain that cause in Britain.

My greatest danger was always tiredness. Upon reflection we took on too much. The team is all worn out. I am worn out. But for all that we have survived – together. It has been debilitating having to bend the truth throughout this job. It has a corrosive quality. But we've been granted this licence to misrepresent ourselves for the sake of journalism and the public interest. It has been a privilege not without huge responsibilities. We employed these methods to get to the truth and to expose injustice and criminality where other means would have failed. Personally, I am glad and relieved that all the masquerading is over.

From the comfortable perch of the safe house I can now reflect on the death threats I have received, the close encounters with fear and the 'There but for the grace of God go I' moments. For the most part I have rebuffed them, but inevitably some of the fear penetrates – in the shape of an unfamiliar noise late at night or in large crowds scanning faces you hope you won't recognize.

There will be new threats to me but more importantly, there are the new challenges ahead. Right now, I've finally got time to reclaim my life. I've got a chance to rest and a chance to play. And now at last I've got a chance to get back to the River.